# A COUPLE FACES DEATH — MY LIFE AFTER ANNE

## Growing in Acceptance and Peace

BILL NERIN

Magic Mountain Publishing Co
PO Box 962 Gig Harbor, WA 98335

Magic Mountain Publishing Co
PO Box 962 Gig Harbor WA 98335
Copyright © 2010 by William Nerin

All rights reserved. No part of this book may be reproduced, stored in a retrieval system, or transmitted, in any form or by any means, electronic, mechanical, photocopying, recording, or otherwise, without the written permission of Magic Mountain Publishing Co.

ISBN: 978-0-9646789-3-4

Printed in the United States of America

# Contents

Appreciation ..................................................................... 4
Foreword .......................................................................... 5
Introduction .................................................................... 6

PART I: A COUPLE FACES DEATH ............................... 9
Chapter 1	Remote Preparation for Dying ................... 11
Chapter 2	Discovering The Cancer ............................ 16
Chapter 3	The Vaccine Decision ................................ 20
Chapter 4	Keeping Family and Friends Informed ...... 25
Chapter 5	Seizing Every Moment ............................... 32
Chapter 6	Wonderful Hospice .................................... 36
Chapter 7	The Final Days .......................................... 41
Chapter 8	The Shock of Death ................................... 50
Chapter 9	The Memorial Gathering ........................... 56
Chapter 10	The Importance of Friends ........................ 60
Chapter 11	The Importance of Pets ............................. 63

PART II: MY LIFE AFTER ANNE .................................. 67
Chapter 12	The Mystery of Sadness ............................ 69
Chapter 13	My Search for Meaning ............................. 72
Chapter 14	The Disappearance of God ........................ 78
Chapter 15	Living in Mystery ..................................... 91
Chapter 16	Three Important Dreams .......................... 96
Chapter 17	What To Do About Death ........................ 101
Chapter 18	Do I Want Another Love? ........................ 112
Chapter 19	Special Reflections and Events ................ 117
Chapter 20	Where From, Where To ........................... 133
Epilogue	Four years and nearly three months
	since Anne died ....................................... 138
About the Author ......................................................... 140

# Appreciation

This book would not be in existence if it were not for several close friends who urged me to write this book. I thank them as they stood by me and continued to encourage me as the months went on. I also wish to thank those who offered me suggestions for improving the book.

I also feel a great sense of gratification in being able to honor Anne by writing and offering our journey to others who may benefit from it.

# Foreword

THIS exquisite book is Bill Nerin's gift to all who experience the dying and the death of a loved one. In deeply honest journal notes and observations, Bill leads us through the experience of loving his wife, Anne, as she is dying and into his life following Anne's death. Wisdom is reflected in the path Anne and Bill chose as they faced the inevitability of Anne's death. Bill's words teach us that death can be faced with courage and growing love and that the time following the death provides challenges to be encountered with as much personal gentleness as possible.

In a culture that rarely teaches the richness of accompanying a loved one as death approaches and then expects (particularly) men to grieve quietly alone, Bill Nerin's beautiful book shows us that the universal experience of dying can be consciously approached and that the time following the death can be a time of continued growth. Words of grief are expressed here with unusual clarity - articulating questions, experiences and insights through the power of love.

As a Clinical Instructor at the University of Washington School of Nursing, as a grief counselor and as a palliative care consultant, I believe this book is exceptional in grief literature - telling the story about the time facing death and the story of life after the death of a loved one. I highly recommend this unique book.

Gerri Haynes R.N.

# Introduction

**T**HIS book is divided into two parts. The first part is about how Anne and I dealt with melanoma cancer and how we lived our lives until her death. It reveals what took place inside each of us, especially how our love grew in the 10 months from the discovery of the cancer until her death.

The second part is about my grieving as expressed in my journal writings. It reflects the ups and downs I experienced and what I have learned from the grieving process so far. Some of my experiences were what I could have guessed; others were totally new to me. My process of grieving is ongoing and I don't know where it will finally lead me, if indeed there is any finality to the impact of Anne's death on my life.

Also included is a DVD. It is Anne speaking to a class of students at Puget Sound University in Tacoma WA. She spoke on July 3, 2005 almost seven months after discovering the cancer. She speaks for 47 minutes describing her journey in facing death. Then she answers questions for about 20 minutes. It was a last minute idea to videotape the session, so the camera was quickly set up and the record button was pushed. It is not a professional production, but an attempt has been made to enhance the audio part of the video for clarity. Even though it is more like a home movie, people who have seen the DVD have been very impressed by what Anne had to say. I hope this will help you experience Anne and her quiet courage.

One of the important things to note is that while there may be some similarities in grieving, grief is quite unique to the individual. The experience is shaped by a myriad of factors: one's upbringing, family culture, religious beliefs, and intensity of the relationship, view of death, economic status, and genetic makeup. Other factors, just as important, are the capacity to feel, to express those feelings to self and to others, to be open and honest, to have a community of close friends, physical health, the presence of a loving pet – these and many others make our grieving experiences unique.

This book is not an instructional manual of how to face death and grieve. It is one couple's journey and one man's grieving that is shared here. It is for you to ponder and glean from it whatever comes to you. You will digest what you read and hear in the DVD, and in the process may be helped in forming your own journey to death and beyond.

## ABOUT KEEPING MY JOURNAL

It might be useful to explain what I mean by writing a journal. In the last 30 years I have found it helpful to write my thoughts, feelings, dilemmas or puzzles when I am moved or disturbed by something. I have never kept a daily diary or journal; I write only when I am emotionally aroused by some event or thought that comes to me that I deem important.

I have found that in the very process of writing I come up with deeper thoughts and insights that I did not recognize before I began to write. Sometimes it is like the hand and pen just take over and run with the original thoughts. I also have found that in expressing my feelings this way, I am relieved of the surface intensity of the feelings, yet, paradoxically, feel a deeper sense of myself. It helps me know myself, and perhaps, become a little wiser.

When I reread my journal after months or a year, I understand better my life's interior journey – how I have progressed, regressed or just remained stuck. This, too, is helpful to me.

My journal has been for my eyes only, and I have felt free to write embarrassing things if I want. Later if I wish to share a journal entry with someone, then I do so. It is a sharing of me.

It is also my opinion that the body, mind, emotions are more connected and integrated with the actual movement of the hand in the writing process. I think this creates an interplay that ushers in new insights. I don't think this would happen if I typed it on a computer. The handwriting is artistic; the typing is mechanical – at least for me.

# PART I
## A COUPLE FACES DEATH

CHAPTER 1

# Remote Preparation for Dying

JOURNAL AUGUST 17, 2005 - 5 A.M.

*"Lying awake, my body embracing the body of Anne, warm, breathing, asleep. I ponder her being. How many nights will I be able to snuggle her, be one with her not only spiritually, but also physically? She is slowly dying of her cancer. How many days do I have with her this way?*

*Then I feel the mixture of fear and sadness, losing her, without her for the rest of my life. I feel sad and fear for how will I be able to get along without her. In 22 days she will be 74. It's hard to write 74 for it seems not true. She has been so energetic in spirit and body. To me she is still good looking and handsome – more like a 60 or 65 year old woman, extremely well preserved. And in five months I will be 80 even though I feel like I'm 65."*

WHILE an exploratory operation on December 15, 2004 announced a death sentence for Anne, our journey in facing death began years before. This preparation had much to do with how our present journey progressed both in practical terms and in our emotional-spiritual terms.

Anne and I prepared for our dying a few years after our marriage in 1982 when I was 56 and she was 52. We talked about it and prepared financially for it by creating a Living Trust. We prepared a Living Will with explicit directions about the use and non-use of life sustaining processes. We discussed the morality of exhausting our financial assets and/or relying on taxpayer's money to keep us alive when it was clear we had reached the end of our lives. We knew most medical expenses are spent in the last years of a person's life. Why should all this money be spent on us when we had reached the end of our productive and enjoyable lives? The words "productive" and "enjoyable" were the clear benchmarks that would tell us our end was near. We felt that our money would be better spent in the behalf of the young, the poor and in making the world just, peaceful and sustainable.

We were very practical. We shopped for the most economical way to have ourselves cremated. We paid $450.00 each to the Kitsap Cremation & Burial Services.

Anne had told her three adult sons we saw death as part of life and thus to be accepted when that time arrived. They offered no opposition to our plans. I had asked one of her sons and his wife if Anne died first, would they be willing to take care of me if needed. I'll never forget that moment. They both cried.

All of our discussions over the years with our mutual agreements and family support took much of the sting out of facing death. We were not experiencing any fear of death itself; we welcomed it whenever it was ready to visit us. It was something more natural than fearful. This does not mean that in the final months Anne did not experience some spurts of fear, but they would quickly recede. There was some fear of nausea as her cancer grew because nausea always seemed to accompany any illness Anne had in her life. As a little girl living in the Philippines, when her father served there in the Army, she contracted some disease that made her nauseous for about a year. She thought this had something to do with this phenomenon of getting nauseous with illnesses.

As the end neared, Anne told me five or six times that she wanted to die. She felt the exhaustion of her energy, her life. She was no longer productive; there was no joy left in her weakened body and mind. Her spirit was lining up with her body and expressed itself in "I want to die." She was withdrawing from the world, her life. She no longer read the paper or listened to the news.

My fears were about what would happen to me without my Anne. I wondered what would give meaning to my life, what would motivate my living. But, of course, these feelings arose after December 15, 2004, the day we discovered her melanoma.

I think one experience reveals how real Anne was in facing her diminishment and final breath, how willing she was to surrender.

I got a call from a woman in the morning exercise class that Anne continued to attend every weekday morning, even though she could not do much in terms of exercise. This was about six weeks before she died. "Bill, have you noticed how Anne is driving?" the woman said. I replied, "No, because whenever we go somewhere I always drive. What's wrong?" Her friend said that the women were concerned because when Anne backed out of the parking lot she drove very wobbly. I thanked her and said I would talk to Anne.

I was anxious about the forthcoming conversation. When Anne returned I told her about the phone call. Anne simply replied, "That's it. I can't drive anymore." I had expected some resistance; I was relieved. "That's it, I can't drive anymore" came out of her in such a matter of fact tone.

I am convinced that our remote preparation for death had a great influence in our acceptance of death as it grew near.

I believe another part of my remote preparation for death was an awareness I had early on in our marriage. It dawned on me that unconsciously I might be holding back fully loving Anne for fear of the pain that would be mine if she died before me. The more I would let myself love her, the greater would be my heartbreak. Consequently I made a very deliberate decision to give myself as fully as my growth would allow in loving Anne.

Over the years I became aware of the love growing. I think that love manifested itself in an experience I had a day before Anne's exploratory operation to see what this bulge was in her groin. I entered this experience in my Journal.

## DECEMBER 14, 2004, TUESDAY

*I woke up in bed lying next to my Anne. And my mind was floating, thoughts were streaming. But then there came this feeling, awareness – an experience that I found difficult to put into words. Of course I was thinking of Anne's operation the next day.*

*The closest I can come to expressing the experience is the word "oneness." It was like Anne and I were one. It was not that I was "one with Anne"; it was just "oneness" I experienced.*

*I told Anne my words couldn't describe my experience. I said that it was a new experience that defied any known words. I said that it was probably like Paul's struggle to describe his oneness with Christ – "I live, not I, but Christ lives in me." It was like he dissolved and was taken over by Christ.*

*The experience was like I dissolved and became a new reality, an "oneness," an "at one" with or in Anne. Yet I was fully aware of the "me" in all this at the same time experiencing just being "one" in, with, through Anne. Anne in me, I'm in Anne – but the experience left out the "in." The simple word "oneness" is the best I can come up with to describe the experience.*

*It was like, no matter where Anne is, or goes as a result of the operation, I am there. It is like there can no longer be any separation no matter what our external mode of life is – here or hereafter.*

*The experience is what others have tried to describe by the words "one with God" although that expression does not describe it. This has got to be the reason that the mystics simply become speechless. The experience transcends the finite construct of "words." It is "unspeakable."*

*May I never lose this experience, - no matter what, Anne is always me and I am always Anne.*

As I look back upon this Journal entry, perhaps this experience reflected a reality that enabled me to give everything I could to Anne from that day until the day she died some 10 months later.

CHAPTER 2

# Discovering The Cancer

IN October and November of 2004 Anne began to feel a bulge on the right side of her abdomen. She began to think that it might be a hernia or something resulting from her hysterectomy the previous year.

After consulting with the gynecologist who performed the operation, we scheduled an exploratory operation for December 15. For whatever reason, the gynecologist invited a surgical oncologist to assist her.

I was sitting in the waiting room awaiting the result of the operation. As soon as the doctor came in I knew the news was not good. She explained to me that they had discovered tumor cells in Anne's lymph nodes in the groin area. She said that the oncology surgeon tried to remove all the cells but that it was difficult to know whether they were all removed as some cells were on the artery. The cells were being examined in the lab to determine the nature of the tumor.

The lab report revealed that it was melanoma. Since there was no primary source discovered for these cells, it was concluded that these cells had migrated to that area in 1971 when Anne had a melanoma on her right leg surgically removed. After five years she was declared clear of the cancer.

Naturally, we were both shocked. Anne always felt that she would die of some other cause.

Just three weeks after the operation Anne began to feel the bulge again. We went to the surgical oncologist and he took a sonogram in his office. Shock was on his face. "I can't believe this has grown back so fast," he said. He was amazed that for 33 years Anne's immune system had kept those cells in check. He explained what Anne could do to help strengthen the immune system. He told us that for the last five years he had attended every seminar he could about the aging process. The thinking is that the way we age is through the diminishment of the immune system. For women, after 35, the system diminishes one percent per year and for men it is one percent per year after 40.

He suggested we look into a vaccine research study being conducted at the John Wayne Cancer Institute in Santa Monica CA. Vaccines boost the immune system. We drove home knowing that time was short and determined to live as fully as we could in the time allotted to us.

My Journal entries of January 26 and February 4 describe my thoughts and feelings after knowing Anne was shortly to die.

### JANUARY 26, 2005 10:25 A.M.

*Anne suggested that I write this. These words cannot convey what I feel and what I can't feel, but nevertheless, it is in me. Anne is gone for her exercise (building her immune system) and for another test at Group Health.*

*I move through the house, kitchen, dining room, halls and office – as if in slow motion. I notice my voice is in slow motion when the phone rings. It sharpens, returns to normal, it has some spring in it when Anne calls.*

*I stop the myriad tasks facing me on my desk to write. There is now a need to write.*

*Lurking in my bowels is a feeling of foreboding. I act more in response to stimuli rather than self start. This slow motion feeling lets me be more in the here and now. Tending to whatever Anne wants, needs, is the overwhelming space I now live. Only the pressing duties pertinent to just living, surviving, demand my attention.*

*I have no care for golf, for Washington Public*

Campaigns[1], my other projects. I even struggle to keep myself in good shape.

There is not much lightness of spirit. Heavy is the word that best fits. Even attention to the "duties of living" only serves as a distraction from this heavy feeling.

I am willing to be where I am now, to be in my present state. It seems to make each moment more important. It makes me more caring and sensitive, less impatient. I just keep moving from one moment to the next, almost as if there is no tomorrow. Setting up future playful engagements seems almost too impractical to make.

Anne is now home.

## FEBRUARY 4, 2005

I wake up and let myself think of my future without Anne. I began to fear – who would take care of me if I were sick in bed, lost my contact lenses in my eye? What community do I really have here?

Then I remember the times in the past when for one reason or another I was filled with fear, panic – felt personally threatened to the point of not being able to think. Anne was always there with me, calming me, being real, offering constructive actions, straightening my confused thinking. Who could I go to around here if that would happen in the future? Who would understand my plight? Who could I trust to share my most vulnerable self in that state?

Then I thought, I had all those resources back in Oklahoma. I was in a community of people that I had no qualms about asking for help, revealing my vulnerable self. I left all that when I married Anne. She became my community. Our resources for each other were the perfect blend, fit.

---

[1] Washington Public Campaigns is an effort in Washington State to pass legislation to have public funding of state-wide elections.

I shared this with Anne in bed. She fully understood my fear. She gently suggested that I needed to take steps to build that community here. But it seems too awesome. How can I have that – it takes years of shared experiences, it takes just the right fit of soul mate-type people. What to do?

## Chapter 3

# The Vaccine Decision

ANNE and I discussed the vaccine research project recommended by the surgeon who operated on her December 15. We set up an appointment with the John Wayne Cancer Institute for February 11 and flew to Santa Monica, CA the day before the appointment.

We discovered that Anne could get into the program provided she underwent another surgery to remove the cancer cells and that a scan be taken two to three weeks later to verify the absence of cancer. It was a double blind research in which one half of the patients would get the vaccine and the other half a placebo. We were told that if the vaccine worked there were only projections as to how long Anne would live or that the cancer would not reappear, perhaps anywhere from five months to five years.

I told Anne the decision was obviously hers to make. I also wanted her to know that I would rather have three to six months of her life in good health to enjoy than to reenter the medical system, be debilitated by the surgery and gamble that she could get into the program and get the vaccine which might lengthen her life as projected. Our oncologist here told us that we should get our most important affairs in order within three months and perhaps we might have three or more months after that: she would project no further.

My feelings at this time are reflected by my journal entry on 2/10/05, the night before we were to meet with the doctor in Santa Monica.

## FEBRUARY 10, 2005, THURSDAY, 2 A.M.

*Before the consultation at the John Wayne Cancer Institute, in Santa Monica.*

*I awake – can't go back to sleep – I'm aware I have been feeling uneasy the past three weeks with the almost frenetic well wishes: "Praying for a miracle," "You can beat this," "You're curable." What I'm uneasy about is that I have not been into that frenzy. I have been ready to accept Anne's death. I have had no prayer of petition to save Anne's life – thus I have been out of sync with all of Anne's friends and some relatives. This has made me feel uneasy. Is there something wrong with me?*

*In bed it became clear to me. Death is part of life. We have got to die sometime, somehow. My prayer has been simply to love Anne, give Anne the best love I have, care for her, tend to her, give her laughs, snuggle often, embrace more, hold each other more, try to be less impatient and grouchy, do what she loves doing. That loving her as she is, from moment to moment, is the best I have to give to her. And since love is part of God, it is God loving her. And I am willing to accept God's plan: to live or die, now, three months, three years – ten years from now – whenever death comes.*

*My fear, anxiety, is more how I will cope with her death, whenever it comes.*

*My uneasy feeling begins to fade. I ponder again how life is a mystery, how mysterious each of us is, how God is mystery.*

*I am consoled by Jesus' prayer – "If possible let this cup pass from me, but not my will but thine be done." I'm willing to surrender to God, to Mystery, to Love. I don't feel I'm doing wrong to Anne, or not loving her, by not praying for a miracle, desperately praying for her to be cured. If anything can help her it's for me to love her just as she is – that will help her immune system. I am being a vessel through which God loves her. God knows I want her as long as I can have her. God knows how I will miss her, struggle without her. I put everything in God's hands.*

*I always have had trouble with prayers of petition. Does God give me what I want or not? What criteria are used? I'm not praying hard enough, I'm not good enough; Anne is not worthy of longer life, etc.? So those prayers ceased to make sense to me. Prayers of gratitude and love fit for me.*

*My love for Anne is the prayer I use. It is my prayer for Anne. I think that those who pray petitions are mainly expressing their love for Anne. For some it may come from their own fear of death. But what I know of Anne, Anne's friends – it is their way of saying to Anne, "We love you."*

*When I shared this with Anne around 4:30 a.m. she totally agreed with me. And our sharing with each other helped us both. Anne mentioned how so much of a person's money is spent on the last months of a person's life – trying to stay alive. How that money could be used for other human needs – for the young, etc. Anne's thought about entering clinical trials is as much to advance the science of cancer cure for those who come after us as it is for her own sake.*

After we came home Anne struggled with the decision to enter the program or not. She knew I would support her either way. Finally on a bright, sunny afternoon on March 1, lying out on the deck with the sun bathing on her and with eyes closed in a prayerful state, a decision came to her - followed by peace. This is her email sent to family and friends on March 2 announcing her decision –

*My dear, dear family and friends.*
*We have had a shift in plans. We mistakenly thought the surgery scheduled for 3/3 to clean out my groin cancer (so I MIGHT be eligible for the vaccine program) was less intrusive and less radical than it, in fact, is. The only*

*reason the surgeon is willing to operate is because I may get into the vaccine program. Otherwise, both surgeons said they would not operate as they expect the cancer will just grow back again.*

*Thus we reassessed the gains and risks involved.*

*After consultations and gathering information, I realized more fully the implications, possible side effects and stress involved in this surgery and recovery process. Then I thought about the gamble I was taking with the vaccine study: 50% get the placebo; if all the cancer can be cleaned out, will it grow back before I can get a readable Cat scan (and thus eliminate me from the vaccine program); only 40-45% of those who get the vaccine live a median five years; there is no information as to how aggressive the cancer was in that 45% population (and mine is very aggressive). All these factors lead me to say for me, the possible gains of surgery and vaccine are not worth the risks, and poor quality of life I would have during difficult surgery and recovery period. If I have three to six GOOD months or more left I want to live them as fully as possible, not taking out time for recovering from surgery.*

*Thus I have decided not to have the surgery and cancervax and let nature take its course. I have agonized over this decision for two days, read reports, talked at great length with Bill and to three trusted MD friends/relatives, meditated, prayed over what was the right decision. Yesterday in prayer it came to me: I should not have the surgery. I was so grateful to find an answer. That conviction has simply grown in me since. There is a huge difference in the peace I feel now and the upset I have been feeling in the last weeks. This is the right decision for me, though it might not be the right decision for someone else.*

*I intend to do all I can to improve my immune system (which, thanks be to God, held off this cancer for 33 years, for which I am deeply grateful!), - exercise, eat and sleep well, lower stress.*

*Every moment is precious. Bill and I dance a lot more after dinner in our dining room, go out to lunch and for walks more often. Son Marc is coming tonight for the weekend; that will be pure joy for us! Celebrating life for however long it lasts is what it is all about!*

*Again thank you for all your support in the various forms it takes. I wish I could respond to each of you individually in written form; just know I respond to each of you in my heart.*

*With a heart full of gratitude and love, Anne*

That peace that Anne described in her email grew in the days and months until her death.

CHAPTER 4

# Keeping Family and Friends Informed

WE never discussed whether to keep friends and family informed about the developments and journey in our lives after we told them about the operation that revealed the melanoma. Anne just went ahead and did it, and I followed in her steps by doing the same with my family and friends. At first, I felt somewhat squeamish about giving them sort of a month-by-month update on our lives with the growing cancer. Even now I can't put my finger on what caused this squeamishness. I never discussed this feeling with Anne. She did it as something normal, so I figured it was my problem and not hers. If she felt good about doing it, that was all that mattered to me.

My squeamishness vanished as so many people in our respective families and among our friends thanked us for doing so. They seemed happy to join us, be with us, in dealing with this illness that certainly had death as its final outcome. They were grateful that we shared the various feelings as well as events in this journey. And this response from our family and friends added to our strength and security. We were not on this journey alone, we were with an extended community, sharing love and concern. Even as I write this, I notice some tears welling up in my eyes.

I post here two samples of the emails sent to our family and friends.

## ON DECEMBER 24, NINE DAYS AFTER THE SURGERY, ANNE EMAILED –

*Praise God – my body CAT scan showed no new primary or new metastasized cancer! This reinforces the idea the primary site was my malignant melanoma in 1971. Apparently the 1971 melanoma metastasized and sent cancer cells to my right lymph nodes 33 years ago. I am so grateful those cells were dormant all this time! Probably due to aging and stress my immune system was no longer able to keep them in check and so out popped the metastasized cancerous lymph nodes.*

*We met with our Group Health oncologist today for the first time (the oncologist who did the surgery was an outside consultant). She reviewed the good news of the CAT scan and said the fact the cells remained dormant for so long is a good sign. She is arranging a PET scan of the groin area to see if there are any cancer cells left in that area.*

*So for now, that's the news from Lake Wobegon. We are so grateful for the current good news. It will surely make our Christmas celebration with Marc and family even more joyful.*

*Heartfelt thanks to each of you for your support, love and prayers. Bill, God (or should it be God and then Bill???) family and dear friends have sustained me through this.*

*Love and a Blessed Christmas to all –*
*Anne*

## PS FROM ME, BILL

*What I am feeling and thinking is some sort of quiet calm together with an edge that keeps me from being overly enthusiastic. For the doctor also said that Anne would always be at risk. And she added that the risk of taking the PET scan could also bring bad news, i.e. that* the cancer had spread and then she would have to tell Anne that "you have an incurable disease."

That, she said, is quite a psychological blow to someone who is feeling so healthy.

Both of us are quite firm in wanting to face the facts. So there was no question about not doing the PET scan.

The end result of all this is that I am more than ever wanting to live more fully each day together with Anne, enjoying our companionship, and each our own individual joys and projects, and letting the tomorrow be what it wants to be. Today is what counts. While we all buy into that philosophy, it has a deeper meaning inside me like I have never experienced before. I like the edge feeling; it keeps me in the moment; I hope I don't lose it. I think it will make me a bit of a better person. I feel more of a part of something greater than me.

## PARTS FROM AN EMAIL I SENT ON AUGUST 8, (EIGHT MONTHS INTO ANNE'S ILLNESS)

I feel negligent in not writing more often about our life.

I have found that being distracted has its positive side as well as the more familiar way to view it as negative. For me, being distracted by doing a variety of necessary and unnecessary things covers the sadness and fear I have about my life after Anne.

Distraction is also crucial for Anne's well being. E.g. yesterday we played nine holes of golf (she riding in a golf cart with a dear friend). At the end of the front nine she decided to continue riding with us as we played the back nine holes because as she said "It is better being out in the fresh air and being distracted this way than going home and being distracted in bed."

I try to stay out of the future as much as I can, e.g. what will happen to me when Anne dies? How will I deal with my sadness in missing Anne? These and other thoughts I try to push to the back for I will have to deal with all this *when the time comes, so why bother with them now? Once is enough. But is this being wise? I guess so.*

*On the day-to-day level, Anne and I note the markers of diminishment. When one more thing that Anne can't do happens we get that momentary jolt – "I'm dying," "you're dying" – that jolt of sadness and fear. We have found that to revisit our decision to accept our death as part of life, to be grateful for what we have now, to be grateful for all of the past – is helpful. It restores peace and the fear slides away until the next jolt.*

*So Anne is going through the stages that so many cancer people do; increased pain with increased medication. We started morphine two days ago, - less energy, less appetite, losing weight and strength.*

*Increasingly my life is taking on the tasks that Anne did: cooking more often under her supervision, cleaning, paying bills, nursing her, reminding her to take her medicine etc. She is still able to socialize for two-hour stints, going to dinners and other social affairs, going to her yoga at times, getting massages etc.*

*She is withdrawing from the world's bad news on TV. Her own tragedy is sufficient to deal with.*

*I marvel at her spunk and spirit. I don't think I would have it if I were in her shoes. She is still thinking of others more than herself, as is her way. I must say that in living with her, most of the time, I have felt deficient compared to her.*

*I love each and every one of you and I know that you are there for me when I need you.*

### BILL

To give you an idea of what was going on in me eight months into Anne's journey into her death and getting weaker each day, I share two Journal entries.

## JOURNAL AUGUST 14, 2005

*It came to me during the night. I wake hearing Anne sick, nauseous, in the bathroom. If I could feel nauseous, I could empathize more with her. Feeling healthy, strong, prevents me from feeling the way she is feeling. I could cast back in memory to times when I felt nauseous, but that memory is still not like the real thing now.*

*Then after I helped Anne back to bed, I drifted to the times I felt weak, vulnerable. I realize those feelings lie just beneath the surface of feeling strong, independent, self-sufficient.*

*Somehow in half dreaming or whatever, I went to the weak side of me. And then I felt a Presence. I was not alone. In the vulnerable feeling I felt a community with the Presence and in my vulnerable feeling I felt peace. It wasn't a feeling of strength, of being strong and self-sufficient. It was a feeling of being very vulnerable with the Presence that brought peace in my weakness.*

## JOURNAL AUGUST 17, 2005 - 5 A.M.
## THE GIFT OF ARGUING

*This morning awake in bed one element of our lives in the past looms before me that I will sadly and fearfully miss – and that is our disagreements. Actually the word disagreement does not fully describe the reality. "Disagreement" means the inability to agree on a matter, a perception, a view, a decision to be made. This is what the going back and forth with our words seems to be. Sometimes these so called disagreements take on a sound and fury as though some eternal truth was at stake. We each hold on to our positions at times as if it were a life or death situation. Sometimes anger and a feeling of not being understood rises above the normal body temperature of 98°. Our voices rise in volume. The tone is sharp edged as our own "clarity" about our position becomes sharper.*

*Then the gift of the moment occurs. As I calm down, (sometimes that takes a day and my ego is not at stake) I accept that what we are holding onto is simply our perception of reality, or better, our perception of some minor or major mystery of life. I realize that my perception could be wrong and that perhaps Anne could be wrong, or we could both be right because we are seeing different aspects of a complicated mystery of some human facet of life.*

*Some of our disagreements are silly, such as those based on memory so beautifully portrayed by Chevalier and Gingold in <u>Gigi</u> when they sing, "I remember it well…"*

*Some disagreements are serious. Some are important like trying to make meaning of what is happening in the world, to our lives, to our concern about peace and human dignity for mankind.*

*But in all these so-called disagreements, disputations, arguments, what is really happening for me is that Anne is adding to my truth, my understanding, my reality. She is giving me a "truth check."*

*As I incorporate her perceptions, viewpoints into mine, I discover a fuller understanding, a fuller truth. And sometimes I discover that my position is simply wrong, unreal. This is perhaps the best gift I receive from her. Her position brings me out of my delusion. It makes me real, honest and a better person for all of that. And sometimes I am the instrument of that gift for her.*

*All this of course is rooted in a profound respect and trust we have for each other. We respect each other's intelligence, moral platform, experience of life and deep love for humanity. We trust the other's integrity and loving capacity. We know that beneath it all there is a deep love for each other even though in the heat of battle it seems long gone. But that love, mysterious as it is, is there. It has grown and deepened over the years of struggling together, disagreeing together, playing together, joking together, romanticizing together, enjoying together, supporting each other in down times and up times, embracing together, being gentle together and admiring each other. Being able to laugh and have good times together has watered the flower of love growing in each of us.*

*So this morning at 5 a.m., as I think of how I depend upon Anne's gift of truth and honesty to me, whether it comes in the form of a fight or just pointing out a grammatical mistake in my writing, I feel sad and fearful knowing soon I will no longer have her giving that precious gift to me that makes me more real, more honest and a fuller human being.*

CHAPTER 5

# Seizing Every Moment

ANNE and I considered the crucial items we needed to accomplish, as we did not know how long Anne would have her energy. Our list comprised reviewing and making final touches to our Family Trust, Living Will, Power of Attorney and our Physician Order for Life Sustaining Treatment (POLST); preparing the Memorial; setting up visits with Anne's brother, sister and three sons and families (all of whom lived out of town), and entering Hospice.

With the rest of our time we wanted to do so many things that gave us joy. As soon as Anne recovered strength from the operation on December 15, we began living our life as fully as possible. We had candle light dinners every night, often followed by dancing on our dining room wood floor. We took a January trip to San Diego staying a night in our favorite Coronado Hotel and played golf for one week. We took two weekend trips to Seattle to "do the town"; took more walks together with our loving black Lab, Daphne, often just holding hands in silence; we played more golf and bridge.

We accepted all the invitations from friends for dinners and other experiences. A memorable time was on a friend's boat, watching at close hand the Tall Ships that came to Tacoma in the summer of 2005. Anne returned to her weekly routine of exercise class, yoga class, prayer group, book group and our <u>Nation</u> discussion group.

Several events are worth telling.

One day, Anne got a call from one of her golfing friends who said that they were scheduled to play the first round match in the President Cup tournament at our golf club. This year the tournament was match play, meaning that one had to beat four opponents to reach the final championship match on May 17.

Anne told her friend that she had not entered the tournament (which was to be played over a period of four to six weeks), "because I'm going to die". Her friend had no idea why her name was on the roster, but why not just play this round and if you want, you could forfeit or withdraw later on. Anne said, "not on your life, if I play, I'm playing to win" – and eventually on May 17 Anne did win the President's Cup championship! In her Day Timer she wrote in big letters "I won." It was such a resounding victory, all the lady golfers cheered "this cancer victim doomed to die" who chose to live as fully as possible until she could do no more.

Another important event was a luncheon that Anne had for her exercise and yoga group. It was a symbol of how Anne was viewing her life at this time. She called it a "Celebration of Life" luncheon. In order to be admitted each guest had to put on a sheet of paper a brief description what she or he was celebrating at this time in her or his life, and if possible to print a picture of themselves on the sheet of paper. Some 50 people attended. Anne made an album of the sheets of paper.

Anne decorated the room with many balloons and secured a barbershop quartet to entertain the guests for the first 20 minutes of the luncheon. After lunch she invited anyone who wished to do so to read his or her statement. Various things individuals were celebrating at this time in their lives were deeply touching.

After this, I put Anne's favorite dance tune on the room's loudspeaker system and everyone danced, including the waitresses, to "New York, New York" sung by Frank Sinatra. It was indeed a celebration of life.

Next we did something that became very important for the entire family.

When Anne's family members made individual plans to visit

Anne, I discussed with Anne the idea of video recording the sessions. She jumped at the idea, so I bought a digital camcorder. My idea was to put the sessions into DVDs through my iMac movie program. When Anne's brother, and then sister came, I simply set the camera on a tripod and let it run.

Each talked about experiences they had growing up with their parents and with each other. They had lots of laughs and a few very teary moments. It was their way of saying goodbye.

When the three sons came together, Anne put large sheets of paper on the dining room wall with the genograms (family trees) of her paternal, maternal and family of origin. The four of them sat at the dining room table as Anne told them how her mother and father were raised, married each other, and had Tommy, Anne and Lissa. Then she described in great detail the story of her life in growing up, including her marriage to their Dad and the early years of their childhood. The sons would ask questions, make comments, and tell experiences and perceptions of their grandparents.

They spent almost the entire day in this activity, filling three DVDs. After Anne's death, for Christmas I gave the sons the set of the DVDs and printed copies of the sheets of the genograms. They each saw them as a wonderful way for their own children, especially when grown, to appreciate their roots and a powerful way to remember their grandmother. I also gave Tommy and Lissa DVDs of their visits.

Toward the end another event moved me to tears.

After Anne died, I found eight gift packages in the laundry room. "What were these?", I thought. When I examined them, I discovered they were gifts for me to have after she died. A friend had come one day when I was gone to wrap them for her.

And three days after the Memorial on October 29, the man who gave us massages showed up at my front door, holding a litre of Glenlivit and a packet envelope. In the envelope were certificates for six massages with her handwritten note "Love forever, Anne." I just cried.

I think we lived as fully as we could in each moment given to us.

About one month before Anne died the first part of my Journal entry reflects this. I titled this entry "In dying We Live".

## IN DYING WE LIVE - SEPTEMBER 11, 2005 – 4:30 A.M.

*It has been 9 months since we discovered the melanoma and Anne is still living. It has been an extraordinary journey. We have learned much and grown greatly these months.*

*What we have experienced is that Anne is not alone in her dying. In a sense, I too, am dying with her. That is, to some degree I am feeling her feelings of fear, sadness, peace and acceptance – I am feeling and thinking along with her in her dying. For example, I feel a loss of energy as she does due to her body shutting down. Of course mine is minor compared to hers. I find myself more fatigued than usual, needing more sleep to recover, as she does. I, too, have lost weight, but not as much as she has. I find it harder to maintain my sense of humor, which is so important to Anne.*

*Yet at the same time we are experiencing a living that is new to us. It is now so clear, the dying is bodily only. The spirit, the love, has blossomed and flourished with a new life, a new quality. In the very midst of the pain, sadness, sporadic fears and confusions, both of us have come alive in a new way.*

## Chapter 6

# Wonderful Hospice

I can't remember how long ago it was when Anne and I read the book <u>Final Gifts</u>[2] written by two Hospice nurses. I think it was in the middle or late 90s. At this moment, I can remember only two specifics about my reaction to this book. The first is feeling that for me it is okay to die. The book seemed to confer a deeper sense of safety and peace about dying. While I had a secure feeling about my dying, as reflected in all the early conversations and planning Anne and I went through, it just seemed that <u>Final Gifts</u> cemented that feeling in me.

The second specific thing I remember is the Hospice nurses discovering why, in the course of dying, many people became irritable, contrary to their normal behavior. This puzzled the nurses. Then they discovered the reason. As the dying person became weaker and more debilitated, the caretakers would do more and more for them in their effort to be caring, helpful and solicitous. It might be such a simple action as holding the cup for them while they drank. But in their loving help for the weakening person, they would unconsciously be doing something that the dying person could do himself or herself. When the Hospice team noted this, they became more careful in letting the dying persons do what they could. And with this, they noticed that outbursts of irritation disappeared — at least that's my memory of what I read in the book.

For some reason, that one specific detail made a powerful impression on me. It made so much sense to me. When we do for others what they can do for themselves, it disempowers them.

The whole thrust in maturing from infancy through childhood into adulthood is to grow into being self sufficient, able to care for oneself, able to assume that responsibility. And as that is achieved, the better a person feels about herself or himself.

How often I have seen a small child snatch a piece of clothing away from a mother with a burst of irritation and put the article of clothing on herself.

As a person on the opposite end of life begins to lose that ability to care for self, it's important to let the person do even the smallest thing possible.

I guess that one little item in <u>Final Gifts</u> stuck with me because I strive to be self sufficient, to solve my own problems; and then when I can't, I seek help from others – at times with reluctance.

Reading this book had convinced Anne and me of the value of Hospice. So one of the first things Anne did after deciding to let the cancer take its course was to investigate when she could get into Hospice.

At first, the Hospice receptionist said that it was too early; Anne wasn't yet eligible. Anne persisted on the phone, asking the person to check her medical records, she was dying, she had a terminal diagnosis. Finally the receptionist said yes, you do fit, you can enter Hospice. Anne shouted "Hooray" over the phone and then both Anne and the receptionist began laughing at rejoicing that she is indeed going to die so she could get into Hospice!

Soon a member of Hospice came to the house and explained to us the services that Hospice would be giving us (note "us." Hospice is concerned about the caregivers of the dying person as well).

I cannot say too much about how wonderful the Hospice experience was. The person on the Hospice team that was most central to us was the nurse who met with us regularly. Whenever a health issue arose, like the swelling in Anne's leg or being nauseous, she was there to consult with us. Sometimes she would advise an appointment with the oncologist; another time to get a lymph massage or to get fitted for a full leg stocking to facilitate drainage of the leg.

I think the second most important person on the team was the spiritual counselor. While I was always present when the nurse visited, I was not present when Anne met with her counselor, unless Anne wanted me to be there.

What was crucial to Anne was to have both these persons mesh with her personality so that she could feel free to share her feelings, as well as her thoughts and questions. The first nurse assigned to Anne was not congruent with her personality. We sweated that one out. We did not want the nurse to feel that there was something wrong with his competency, or that it would diminish him with his superiors. We just didn't know how to handle this, but I could tell that Anne was very concerned.

Luckily, Anne had a good friend who was the chaplain at another Hospice system. When Anne presented the problem, her friend reassured her that this problem does arise sometimes. Hospice is aware of this and it is perfectly normal to ask for another nurse. It is important that the two personalities fit each other. Being reassured, Anne consulted with her Group Health spiritual counselor. She told Anne the same thing as her friend had told her. So Anne asked for a change of nurses and we got just what the "doctor ordered." They hit it off so well and intimately.

Our new nurse had a sense of humor and ease that went along with Anne's persistent questions about medications possible side effects and other concerns. Anne was a person who wanted to know everything there was to know about the things affecting her life. In the 10-month period following the diagnosis, I think she must have read or scanned some 10 to 15 books in pursuit of knowledge.

When the nurse visited, or we would go to the oncologist, Anne always wanted me to bring a yellow pad to record all pertinent information about her treatment, progress, tests and medicines. Anne, of course, had her yellow pad as well.

Toward the end, when Anne was very weak, our nurse came on her routine visit. This time Anne was stretched out on the couch in her office with pen and yellow pad in hand. They were discussing a possible new medication. Anne began writing slowly, asking the nurse to repeat what she was saying, struggling to understand and write it down. Then suddenly, Anne threw her pen and yellow pad down and with a weak laugh and smile on her face said, "Why do I need to know this, I'm going to die." Both of us broke out laughing with Anne. All three of us felt so relieved that Anne had decided it was no longer necessary for her to know everything about this medicine. Relief and peace came to Anne in that moment. The three of us cheered. It was another stage of acceptance of her condition, which brought peace.

Our nurse was one of the speakers at Anne's Memorial, her words reflecting the bond that eased Anne's journey to death. The fit of personalities between patient and nurse is so very important.

### HERE ARE HER WORDS AT THE MEMORIAL –

*Dear Bill,*

*Thank you for asking me to share some of my thoughts regarding the time I spent with Anne during the last few months of her life.*

*I firmly believe that it is the responsibility of a nurse to empower each patient, by teaching and providing information that will allow individuals to make knowledgeable and appropriate decisions for themselves.*

*So, for me Anne was the perfect patient. She seemed to have an innate understanding of my role and utilized it fully. She had an unquenchable thirst for "the details," and found comfort in being able to understand and visualize the likely progression of events in the weeks preceding death. Anne always asked and valued my opinion, but made decisions for herself; and thankfully, she was very gracious when I didn't have all of the answers.*

*Anne had a wonderful sense of humor. No matter how serious the nature of our discussions, there was often opportunity to reflect on the light side. Being as Anne was extraordinarily drawn to detail, we often chuckled when I would ask if she could summarize her thoughts and observations at the end of a visit. The difficult and sometimes absurd attempt to implement a medical model of comfort into what is most decidedly a spiritual and emotional experience, often led to laughter. What an enriching experience this was for me.*

*Anne told me her desire was to do everything she could to make her dying and death a positive experience for her family. She only spoke of her work or accomplishments when asked, and the answers were always brief. The experiences that she loved to share were of time spent with family in conversation and life review. We both shed tears of joy as she told of Bill planning a birthday celebration with her sons, even though it wasn't her birthday, and of a special time she spent talking to her grandson. She often said she was so grateful for the time she had to prepare for death, as it gave her an opportunity to share her experience and receive support from family and friends. What courage it takes to face the dying process, with all of its uncertainties, with this utmost bravery and dignity.*

*Anne, by her example, was a vibrant reminder that life, even when shadowed by sickness, is meant to be lived. Anne, the teacher, taught me, the hospice nurse, a great deal about dying. Her lessons on sorrow, strength and acceptance will not be forgotten. As I say goodbye to Anne, I gratefully accept the wisdom and insight that she has offered me, and while I hold these gifts close to my heart, I also bear the responsibility passing them to others who face the same journey.*

*My best to you and your family.*

CHAPTER 7

# The Final Days

ON September 27, a long time friend, Madeline Sue Pryor came to visit us. She was a nurse, now retired, who spent her last professional days teaching at the University of Oklahoma Health Science Center in Oklahoma City. Anne and I knew that Madeline had come to Seattle several years before to stay with a friend who was dying of cancer.

In August, I had asked Anne what she thought about requesting that Madeline come and stay with us as she had with her friend. Anne jumped at the idea; what a relief it would be to have a nurse live with us through the final days of Anne's life. I called Madeline and she said she would be happy to do so when "the time was ready," i.e. when Anne was diminishing enough so as to need constant help.

In September, Madeline was on the West Coast visiting friends and paid us a visit before going back to Oklahoma. After half a day with us, she turned to me and said, "Bill, the time has come. I'm staying."

Madeline noticed that Anne was anxious about her medications and nausea. She also noticed that I was not getting out as I was now caring for Anne around the clock. Madeline felt that she could help both of us. As I had moved from day to day being with Anne in her daily diminishment, I had become accustomed to her condition and had lost a more objective picture. Madeline's fresh eyes and experience told her "the time has come." Madeline was right. Seventeen days later, Anne died.

What a relief it was to Anne and me to have a 24-hour nurse

friend living in our house. Anne emailed friends and family saying, "An angel of God has been sent to us…" Not only were Madeline's technical skills helpful, but being able to talk about Anne's condition and needs was a quiet support for Anne and me.

Anne now spent more time in bed, withdrawing even more from the world and family. However, when someone would call her or come to visit, she rose to the occasion and spoke in a voice strong and energetic. Then she would slump back into her weakness, exhausted by the encounter she had so thoroughly enjoyed.

On October 3, I was working in my office on the second floor of our house. It suddenly dawned on me that while her brother and sister, and her three sons and their families had come and to say their goodbyes, we hadn't.

This awareness shocked me. Madeline was gone from the house for several hours; it was about 11 a.m. I quickly left my desk and went downstairs to our bedroom. I said, "Anne, you have said your goodbyes to the family, but we haven't said ours." She weakly replied, "Oh, that's right. We need to do that."

I helped Anne onto the couch in the living room, ran upstairs, got my iPod and stuck a mike into it and set it on the coffee table next to the couch. I sat on one end and Anne, lying down on the rest of the couch, spoke in her weak voice.

She began by explaining how important it was for her to have known me first as a friend. After her divorce, she had felt so deeply the pain of betrayal that she believed she could never trust or love another man.

(Anne's feeling of betrayal stemmed from her personal meaning of marriage. Anne's meaning was, among other things, a commitment for life. And I suspect her meaning also included some flavor of "it can always be worked out." I think it was a meaning that fit for her, not necessarily for others. Thus she lived a life of marriage some 28 years with that meaning embedded in her mind and soul. Thus, she felt it as a betrayal.)

I took that in; but because I had never experienced a deep betrayal in my own life, it was hard for me to tune into the depth of that feeling. I just accepted that she had been in the deepest of pain.

She said that as she got to know me better as a friend she began to trust me. And as that trust grew she felt safe to love me.

After that opening comment, we talked about how wonderful our life had been together; we laughed at the fierce arguments we had and how we always resolved, if not the subject of the argument, at least ourselves. Sometimes the resolution was in simply accepting whatever was bugging us about the other person was due to our own makeup and upbringing. We knew that whatever it was, "it" was quite secondary to the love we had for each other and all the things we valued together and enjoyed together.

## I THOUGHT BACK TO A JOURNAL ENTRY I HAD MADE APRIL 8, 2005.

*This morning I woke after what seemed like an endless night of dreaming. Lying next to Anne, I had an experience that carried with it an awakening. It was a new experience and I am sure the following feeble description will in no way explain the experience. I felt transformed, made whole, quite like I had never felt before. I felt loved for every little aspect of me, for all my defects, scars, liabilities, past sins and defections as well as for all my strengths. That feeling of love came to me through another human – my Anne.*

*It is Anne who loves me so. Since Anne's discovery of the cancer in her groin, I have been aware so often of Anne's total love for me. It has struck me as only mysterious, this kind of love. Over and over with tears in her eyes and softness and tenderness in her voice she has told me how much she loves me. Never before in our life together has she seemed to utter those words with so much affection, so much thoroughness. Her body, face, embrace, words, conveyed to me that there was nothing about me not loved, embraced. That may be foolish on my part to say, for I know some of my traits and actions annoy and upset her. But it is like those very warts are not only part of me but in some way they are weaved into my tapestry in such a way as to add beauty to the whole picture. It is like my "negative" actions and traits do not stand separate in me worthy of criticism and blame. Rather they are part and parcel of my living, moving, evolving life, personhood. Keep them separate, cut them from me, and I am not I. And it is the "me" that Anne loves, not just a magnificent or annoying aspect. It's the complete package that makes me, me. Oh, I'm sure that my positives in her eyes far outnumber the negatives. But the experience of "love for me" I experienced this morning went beyond all traits. It went to my core, my core out of which any traits, behavior comes.*

*I believe it is the basic core residual in every human being in the world – a human core that wants to be loved and that wants to love. It is from this core that all else springs. It is this core that is lovable, even if covered by the sins and brutality of 50, 60, 90 years of human living. This morning the love I felt was not just for my core, it was for it and all that has emerged from it. The whole, integrated, me. The weaving of both sound and weak threads of cotton or wool – was being loved by Anne. Is such a love human, or is it only the love God can give and has? I believe it is both. God does not only love me through Anne, but that kind of love has become part of Anne too. I don't know if Anne loved this way early on in our lives, or that Anne can love anyone like she can love now. It seems to me that the seed of God – love, has grown in her, taken her over so now it is Anne, as well as God who loves me so completely. And also it is through Anne that God touches me, loves me.*

*Being so loved is to be subsumed into another and by another. A bond, union, oneness is created so that it feels permanent. So when Anne dies first or I die first – we are still one in love. Now I suspect if I had kept all I had ever written or said I would find the same words as written above. The words are not the experience. You can't "teach" this by words for words can't convey the experience. Only the experience can convey the experience. I think this is akin to what Thomas Aquinas said at the end of his life – all that he had written in his life was but straw.*

*So the real teacher, the real human developer is to love someone totally or in such a way that a person ends up feeling totally loved. Is this not the reason that children, grown sons and daughters feel so wonderfully bonded with their mother, because mothers can give that kind of love to their offspring? On the other hand, is this not why a child, son, daughter can feel so alienated, filled with anger, hatred, even toward a mother if that child feels unloved by its mother? The need is so strong, that if not received, the reaction is equally strong.*

*No wonder the best teachers that taught the most important lessons are the teachers that somehow conveyed to the student "I love you," "you count." And that most important lesson is "Gee, I'm loved, I'm lovable, I count." That one lesson learned in a fourth or seventh grade class from one particular teacher is the most important thing the child will ever learn in school! It is transforming and unleashes the entire human potential in the child. It is the child's "resurrection."*

We talked for about 40 minutes then Anne felt so weak she had to stop. She said "let's continue later." We never did get around to finishing whatever was left unsaid. Perhaps we both realized we had said it all in 40 minutes.

In the two weeks before October 9, Anne had said to me five or six times, "I want to die." On Saturday, October 8, Madeline and I had to be away from the house, so I asked a friend to sit with Anne while we were gone. Sometime after Anne died, he told me that she had come into the living room to visit and had told him she wished she could have an embolism and die.

On Sunday, October 9, Anne woke up with a headache and feeling nauseous. At 2 p.m., Madeline took Anne's temperature. She had a fever. Madeline called Hospice and they ordered a prescription. I was playing golf and Madeline called me on my cell phone to come home. I hurried home and went to the druggist to get the medicine. In the late afternoon, I was in the bedroom with Anne and noticed a slight movement of her body that suddenly broke into an uncontrollable shaking with her eyes rolling around. I screamed for Madeline and she and Linda, (our daughter-in-law who had just arrived from Winthrop, WA,) rushed in. Anne was having a grand mal seizure. I had never witnessed such a seizure before and was scared out of my wits. Madeline calmly said "This will end." I was so relieved. When the seizure stopped, Anne was in a coma.

We called Hospice and the duty nurse said to call 911 to take Anne to the ER.

How professional, how calming, how thorough the Gig Harbor Medics were in taking care of Anne. They asked if Anne had a POLST (Physician Orders for Life-Sustaining Treatment) and I gave the form to them. They securely fixed it onto Anne's body to make sure it would go everywhere she went. POLST was her signed written instructions against life sustaining interventions. (Later the family wrote to the Medics at the Fire Department to thank them and comment on the superb way they treated Anne, and the way they cared for her distressed family.)

We followed Anne to the ER at Tacoma General Hospital. The Emergency Department was like a traffic jam. We located Anne and encountered a most sympathetic nurse who shared the story of her mother in a similar situation.

After what seemed like a time longer than I am sure it was, the ER doctor came out and asked for me. He said that Anne had an extremely high temperature which might be caused by an infection and said he could administer a massive amount of antibiotics to see if that would take care of the infection. He said that he had read the POLST with its instructions. He wanted to verify that the directions on the POLST reflected our present wishes. I said yes. He gave me a look that said; "OK it's your decision." Later as I reflect on this reaction I realize he was only making sure that he was doing what we wanted.

Anne spent the rest of the night at the hospital. Monday, she was taken to a residential Hospice unit. The physical layout and attitude of the staff there so symbolized the difference between the ordinary medical system which is designed to save lives and the Hospice system dedicated to helping the dying person have a peaceful and pain-free death.

In just 24 hours Anne had been removed from the familiar peace of her home to the ER room, to another room in the hospital, then to the Hospice residence. Within 24 hours Anne and we encountered the staff of the Medics and the ambulance, the doctor and nurses of the ER, the medical personnel on the upper floor of the hospital and finally another set of doctor and nurses at the Hospice residence. In the hospital I heard the doctor prescribe a medicine different from what Anne was taking. The same thing occurred at the Hospice residence.

At the residence they had a lovely bedroom next to Anne's so that I could hear anything that Anne did. She was still in a coma. I went to bed exhausted that Monday night. It was a terrible night for me. Here is what I wrote the next morning.

## OCTOBER 11, 2005 - AT THE FRANCISCAN HOSPICE CENTER, 7:00 A.M.

*I awoke at 4:30 a.m. hearing Anne breathing phlegm. I was surprised to wake so early since I was so exhausted when I went to bed at midnight. I thought I would sleep longer. I tried to go back to sleep, but I began to think. I was disturbed; I felt I was losing control. I felt that by moving Anne here I unwittingly turned her over to another network of doctors, nurses, and hospice workers. Tacoma General was one turnover, now 24 hours later another turnover. I had lost our Group Health nurse as being in charge, – who had grown so close to Anne, admiring her, learning from her. I felt the loss. Our nurse is no longer in charge / another hospice nurse. Damn! I hate it.*

*Here, there is a new doctor in charge. Do they give their own different meds? Is Group Health Hospice still in control or the Franciscan staff at this place? I'm not at ease. I am very upset, disturbed and fearful – almost in a panic.*

*One good thing from this being out of control is being one with Anne who has lost control of her former life, her being so much in charge at times, relying on me for feedback to her, helping her be clear about her decisions whereby she is in control. Now she is totally out of control, in the hands of others. I am her main hand to protect her, see to it that her wishes are fulfilled.*

*I hear of changes made; for example, no more Decadron. How did that happen? - "It was your orders. Mine?" I never gave that. What the hell is going on? So many different systems – medics from 911, ER Tacoma General, room 604 staff at Tacoma General, Group Health Hospice, now here. So many different voices. At times I think decisions are made and we are not told what and why. They whisper, in secret conspiracy so I won't know what they are saying.*

*Am I being too finicky, paranoid, afraid, jealous of being in charge of my love, Anne? So, as with Anne I feel out of control. Should I just accept it? Surrender? Is that good or bad? I would feel so bad, so much a failure, if I don't do my duty of love and protect Anne, care for her dying wishes.*

*I also resent the presumption of people calling, coming unannounced, uninvited. Am I not in control, should I not welcome all these invasions by friends of Anne? Sure, have at her. I think of the hoard of black-clad Greek women in <u>Zorba the Greek</u>, eager to pounce on the French woman's dying. Of course all of this is insane, non-applicable. But it reveals how I feel.*

*Am I screaming, acting like a petulant child? Let go Bill; welcome the friends. Give up possessing Anne, let go.*

It was a frightening night for me. As soon as possible I called our Group Health nurse and said, "Who is in charge of Anne?" Of course I wanted our Group Health nurse. I was so unbelievably relieved when she said that she was! She came over that morning and I saw her in action, checking the records, making sure the meds were the ones that had best fitted for Anne. (Even now as I write this, it is as if I am reliving the whole scene again – I feel the same relief again as if the Group Health nurse was back in charge. My feelings are so strong that if I could, I would call her and just tell her how much she meant to Anne and me. Tears are in me.)

Tuesday, Perry, the youngest son from California arrives. He went over to Anne who had not responded to anything except a few grimaces when she was turned or bathed by the staff. (I had set up some of Anne's favorite music CDs to play beside her bedside in hopes she could hear them and be soothed.) Perry says, "Hi Mom, it's Perry", Anne turns her head and slightly smiles. Perry says, holding her hand, "Mom your smile means so much to me." On Wednesday Marc, the middle son comes and Perry says "It's Marc." Marc goes to the bed and with a smile Anne turns her head; Marc leans over to hug her and Anne raises her arms. Those were the only two responses to people from Anne that I saw before she died. The sense I make of this is that this reveals the powerful connection between mother and child.

CHAPTER 8

# The Shock of Death

ON Friday, October 14, Anne's sister Lissa and I are standing around Anne's bed around 7:30 a.m. Anne is silent. Lissa and I are quietly talking and lightly petting Anne. At 8 a.m. I notice that Anne had stopped breathing. Previously, one of the nurses there had told me about a resident who had stopped breathing for about two and one-half minutes and then began breathing again. So I waited and timed Anne's lack of breathing. I didn't want to be an alarmist and get the nurse if this was only a spell.

After 30 seconds I went out to the nurse's desk and told the nurse that Anne had stopped breathing.

The nurse came in and listened with her stethoscope to Anne's heartbeat. I was standing right next to the nurse. She put down the scope, turned to me and said, "She's dead." At that moment I felt like something had been jerked right out from my stomach; it was a visceral feeling, experience. The nurse left and I asked Lissa if I could be alone with Anne.

When they left, I began to cry, sobbing and stroking her warm body. I kept saying over and over through my tears, "I can't believe it, I can't believe it." At the same time there was a voice in my head that said, "You know you have prepared for this, you know she was going to die," yet that voice had no power over me: I just kept crying and saying out loud "I don't believe it." It seems like this went on for about 15 minutes. It may have been more or less; I did not clock it. When my crying stopped, I quietly repeated over and over, "I love you so much" and continued to pet her, loving her.

Anne's body was still warm and I thought that I should bring Lissa in to have some alone time with Anne. While Lissa was with Anne, I went to the small chapel-like room and paced; quietude and peace came over me and I was able to be glad for Anne that her journey was finally over. After a time, I went back into the room and Lissa and I just hugged each other.

Later, I tried to piece together why I kept saying, "I can't believe it" when for 10 months we had been preparing for this. Was it just the shock? Was it that no matter how much I had thought I accepted Anne's dying there was still a strong piece of me that did not want her to die? Or was it just my cry over the death of a loved one? Was it my last gasp to hang on to her? Or was it my way to say "I love you so I don't want you to go"? I think the visceral jerk of something from my guts was a part of me that died. Yet I do not know what it was all about. Life is a mystery and so is death.

I include here four short Journal entries that reveal what was going on inside me the days right after Anne's death.

## OCTOBER 16, 2005, SUNDAY, 7 A.M.
## TWO DAYS AFTER HER DEATH

*Oh my love – let me know you are okay – in peace and happiness. Somehow let me know. I love you so and I am so heavy in heart.*

*I opened one of your gifts this morning – a beautiful shirt. Your taste was so good. I love how cultured you were and at the same time so very, very earthy. You could cuss right along with soaring to a Mozart piece of music. No one like you. I so miss you.*

*Yesterday was our anniversary. I thought of it as I awoke, couldn't think of a way to celebrate it, then got distracted the rest of the day with family, duties, and watching Southern California and Notre Dame play football. So as I write this I am so sad that I cannot love you* in marriage anymore. It's like I want time to have stopped months ago when you were still fully alive and active and full of energy – your old spirited self.

Now, from wherever you are, however you are, help me live without you and your body. Help me down this sad, heavy path ahead of me.

In a way I cherish my sadness and heavy heart, because it's my love for you. I never want to lose my love for you. Can I ever be joyful again and still feel this love, which is bound to sadness, which I have for you? Can I feel my love for you, bound to a joy, as well as I now feel my love for you? Oh, be with me; let me experience you.

### OCTOBER 17, 2005, 6:40 A.M.

I'm shaving; no one's standing at Anne's sink – never more will Anne be there.

Then it hit me, such a simple truth. Why had I never seen this before with such clarity and force as I was seeing it now? Anne's spirit, her energy, her love, her generous accepting soul, was all manifested, felt through her body – the presence of her body. Earlier after her death, on October 14 I had beseeched her to show her presence, her spirit to me in a way I could feel it. "Let me know you are really with me still – not just relying on unfelt faith," simply believing she was still in me and part of me.

Then I thought, - God manifested God's self through the body of Jesus. Through the body of Jesus the followers could feel God, experience God. Then Jesus died. His friends and loved ones wanted his spirit, his soul, his invisible love energy to be made present and felt as they had before through his body. As they laid the body in the grave and rolled the stone before it, they were so deeply sad – they could not experience, feel that inner-presence through the senses of hearing, seeing, touching, smelling as they had before because that spirit was part of the physical body.

Then three days later something happened – somehow

*without the body, they were able to experience the invisible soul, spirit of that love, acceptance, peace, gentleness, that they had experienced through the physical means of his body. That's what I want from Anne, to still experience her in a new way – her spirit to my spirit. For now I only experience her when something hits my eye, affects my nose, moves my ear in sound – that reminds me of her, be it the song "New York, New York" or the smell of her perfume or that sink with no one now standing before it.*

*This morning I left the door from the living room to our bedroom open – when Anne was here, Daphne, our precious loving Lab, would always lie before the door closed, awaiting Anne. Today, door being opened, Daphne simply sat there, partially in the hall behind the door and looked up to me writing this in the dining room. I felt so sad; I went to pet her and hold her and told her "Anne's not here." Daphne was missing the spirit of Anne's presence manifested through her body. I'd be jealous if Daphne ever experienced Anne's bodiless energy and spirit in her Black Lab body and I didn't!*

## OCTOBER 22, 2005, 12:15 P.M.

*I've been going through Anne's papers, folders, desk, trying to discover what I need to know for now, and to put some order out of her scattered piles of stuff. I come across things that make me remember her, think of her, ponder her. Throwing away so many sheets of paper, cards, notes galore, feeling like part of me is leaving. I feel very heavy and sad.*

*I wonder – after the memorial and tidying up her affairs, will I have any meaning to live? What I am doing now for the memorial and thereafter is really an act of love for her, honoring her, pressing her to my heart. But when it is all over, will there be anything more to live for? I can see more clearly than ever how she was a source of life for me. Our interacting love and life together sustained her and me, made our life so joyous and spirited, a life worth living. What will happen to me in the days ahead?*

*To survive, find a life, must I distract myself from thinking of her, loving her? Will my activities subtly take my mind off of her? Do I want that? How can I keep remembering her, having her in my heart, and still go on? What secret will I find to this dilemma?*

*I don't want to become less loving a person, becoming more self-interested and absorbed. My life with her has opened my heart to a deep loving capacity. I really do feel that I have grown less selfish, more spontaneously generous. I don't want to lose that. How can I keep growing in love?*

## OCTOBER 23, 2005 – 6 A.M.

*I have accomplished my last task of love of Anne. I have cared for her through her illness and death giving her my all, my complete undivided attention. In the last four weeks, except for a few rounds of golf while others attended Anne, I was with her. At the last, I was at her side during her last breath.*

*During the last months of illness she wanted me to be with her more and more. It seemed that while my specific acts of help were important to her, it simply was my presence that counted most. That was our way of love. We never spoke about being so present! We just knew that that was what we both wanted.*

*After such loving, what else could there be for me? The final days of love were the greatest pinnacle of my life. To tend to her, to love her this way felt so pure for me, so totally giving, totally unselfish – what greater love could I ever achieve? I've reached the peak of my life; anything else is nothing but vapor. I feel my soul has gone, my spirit is gone. I'm only biologically living.*

*The final chapter of my love is the Memorial Gathering and settling the estate for her - perhaps also the DVDs for the Christmas presents – then it is time to join my Anne, my love. Anything else on earth seems so empty, worthless. Oh Anne, where are you? I'll come to you.*

CHAPTER 9

# The Memorial Gathering

ONE of the tasks that Anne and I had noted on our priority "to do" list was to plan for the funeral. We had both been raised in institutional religions, she as an Episcopalian and I as a Catholic. But as we had grown older we felt that we did not need to attend church to worship God or to sustain our faith in a God. We felt that we worshipped God when we were awestruck by the beauty of a rainbow, the majesty of Mt. Rainier, the love of people, the laughter springing from a light heart, the ability to accept and laugh at our limitations, the beauty of man made creations such as an El Greco painting, a Mozart composition, the grandeur of an ancient cathedral, an opera, ballet, poem, a dinner created by Anne's culinary imagination and the simple beauty of our home built by the artistry of son Marc.

All these things created such good feelings within us that it offered us daily opportunities to be grateful to God for all the beauty, all the goodness and all the struggles to be better people.

To love others was to love God, too, for we believed that God is in each person; to be loved by others is to taste the love of God for us.

In our later years, I guess you could call Anne and me "non-institutional Christians" (NIC). We believed that Jesus was a unique and special gift from God to show us a way to love and be in peace. We tried to love the enemy as Jesus taught, even though at times it was tough. We always felt unfinished in our human development but that each day offered to us another opportunity to love, be grateful and to improve. Before Anne died she was able to say, "I have no regrets."

So given our backgrounds and our present state of being we tried very hard to determine how the funeral should be.

Anne went a couple of times to Episcopal services, but that left her wanting. We went to the Catholic Worker House in Tacoma for their weekly potluck supper and Eucharist conducted by one of the young Jesuit volunteers. It was so simple, so full of community sharing and love that it touched our hearts. But we recognized that to be authentic we had to become part of that living community of personal service to the poor, sick and homeless in that section of Tacoma.

Anne did set aside a saying, a poem or two and some music that she wanted to be played at the funeral. I got a charge out of her selection – "The 12$^{th}$ Street Rag," "The Entertainer," "New York, New York" and "III Valse/Allegro Moderato" from *Tchaikovsky's 5$^{th}$ Symphony*. It so well reflected Anne's love for the sublime to the bawdy and to the swing of dancing.

She asked her brother, the historian in her family, to draft an obituary we could work from. Beyond that we never could seem to finalize anything.

So after her death I just decided to design the Memorial and find a place for it. What emerged from my unconscious mind was a key concept – community. It was in various communities in Gig Harbor that we each moved, loved others and received love back. It was the community of Anne and me, then of the extended family, then all of the groupings that we lived out our lives in close to home. In these various communities be they of exercise, or fun and games, or serious discussion of thoughts and viewpoints, or of prayer Anne and I were nourished.

So it was fitting that the Memorial be as much a community event as possible with as many active people as possible. I named it a "Memorial Gathering." I chose "gathering" rather than service because it sounded less pretentious to me, more human and therefore looser and inviting and admissible to human failure. This would not only be something to celebrate and remember

Anne, but it would be a celebration for the community itself. I think that is what happened.

After looking at various sites that we could rent and that would give us a feeling of community, we chose a small Lutheran Church just a half-mile from our home. The small sanctuary had movable chairs set in a semi circle that would hold about 200 people. That would make us feel less formal than rigid pews and be more inviting for people to stand up, to see each other and share memories – a community gathering of memories and love. From the seating area you could see the light airy outside world of nature through huge windows, which lifted one's spirit. The inside walls and paneling of wood gave off a warm feeling. The church was just right for what we wanted. The staff at Agnus Dei Lutheran church was very welcoming and helpful.

In the Memorial program I tried to cover the essential parts of Anne's life. Under the title of "Memories" I listed the following:

Growing up with Anne - (her brother)
Growing up with Anne, our Mom - (one of her sons)
Growing up with Anne, our Grandma - (a grandson)
Knowing Anne as a friend - (a close friend)
Knowing Anne as a professional - (a colleague)
Knowing Anne in her final illness - (the nurse)
Knowing Anne for 23 years - (her husband)

Each of the seven speakers spoke for no more than three minutes, but they were impactful, funny, loving and set the tone for others among the more than 225 attendees sharing their memories.

The sharing covered the whole range of human aspects of life, from the poignant to the earthy. For example, one woman, a long-time colleague in our professional careers as family therapists, told about when she first met Anne. It was at a three-week training session conducted by Virginia Satir[2] in a rustic boys

---

[2] Satir was one of the pioneers of family therapy that emerged in the late '50s in the U.S.

camp in Marin Co. CA. She bunked with several other women in a bare dormitory bereft of toilet, showers and washbasins, which were located in a common area some yards away from the dormitory. As she and Anne were leaving the dormitory after breakfast, Anne said she needed to pee. The speaker thought she was headed for the building with the toilets; but no, Anne simply dropped her pants, squatted and peed on the ground.

Everyone just howled. The story was so typically Anne, the refined Ph.D. who loved the fine arts was about as down to earth as you can get.

Members of Anne's various communities produced the Memorial Gathering. They helped set up the chairs, fix and serve the food after the program was finished, provide the music, create picture boards of Anne's life for display, administer the guest book, record the event and help with restoring the church after all was done.

Several people said this was the best funeral they had ever attended; some said that this is what they want for their funeral. I definitely got the impression that they were absolutely sincere and not just giving a nice compliment to me. I felt that we had given Anne a great send off to her new existence, and that it had given all of us a chance to express our love and appreciation for Anne as well as for the human community.

## CHAPTER 10

# The Importance of Friends

**O**UR friends, some life long and some recent, were extremely important to us. The essential reality was the powerful love that penetrated the body and soul of each of us, manifested in enthusiastic willingness to help us with any need. It manifested itself in gracious smiles, rejoicing in our enjoying the remaining days of our life together. We were constantly amazed by how thoughtful our friends were in detecting what would give joy to Anne – whether it was a dinner, sailing to see the Tall Ships, a game of bridge, an invitation to stay overnight with friends in Seattle, to visit the Japanese garden, to go to the symphony.

What signified the sincerity of their friendship was how easy it was in asking for their daily help as Anne grew weaker.

This part of my Journal entry that I wrote about five weeks before Anne died expresses my thoughts and feeling about this love given to us by all our friends and family.

### IN DYING WE LIVE - SEPTEMBER 11, 2005 – 4:30 A.M.

*Anne and I are discovering an enormous outpouring of love, not only from within our own hearts, but from the hearts of so many friends and family members. It seems that dormant love has exploded all over the place.*

*Why is this? I can only fathom several possible explanations. One is that Anne herself has been and is a very special person – thoughtful of others, vigilant and helpful when others are in need. She has a great energy of discovery, adventure and joie de vivre. She is scrappy and fun loving and has a rebellious side in her that sparks surprises in life and a new way of seeing things. As a result, many people are attracted to Anne and love her.*

*This does not mean that Anne is perfect and doesn't have her faults and limitations. It doesn't mean she doesn't make mistakes. But I must say that in living with her for 23 years, I have never detected a thread of meanness in her soul. I can say that with some authority, as I know what meanness is. I have several threads of meanness in me that sneak out at times and I must wrestle with these demons to hold them in check. But I have never detected any such threads in Anne. If anything, one of her faults is that at times she is too "helpful," too "thoughtful" and some, including myself, find it irritating. "Let me navigate for myself" is my reaction, "don't impose yourself so much." But of all the faults to have, that is not a bad one, is it?*

*But even with her faults, she has had the marvelous ability to recognize them and to accept them as part of her when she is unable to change the faults, as she would desire.*

*So part of the explanation of this explosion of love is that Anne is so easy to love. Another factor is simply the fantastic capacity people have to love. That love may be dormant or at least not so evident until something like Anne's dying comes along. Then the deep love in other people's hearts springs alive and becomes manifest. It is so overwhelming that Anne seems to be crying everyday at someone's act or expression of tenderness.*

*And love is contagious, too. I, for one, have noticed that I have softened and grown in love for certain people who in the past have irritated me because of mannerisms they have. As they have shown care, attention and love to Anne, that love has helped me increase my love for them. Yes, love is contagious. It only validates an old belief I have in non-violence, namely that the way to deal with violence is simply to love the violent-acting person – as hard as that may be. I believe that only love can dissipate hatred and violence. The fact that love is contagious is another explanation why Anne and I have been experiencing this explosion of love.*

*Finally I suspect that another reason for this explosion of love is that Anne decided not to try various possible medical experiments such as cancer vaccines or interferons to prolong her life. Her life these past months has been an announcement – death is natural, death is part of life, death is not to be feared. And in our culture, so afraid of death, this announcement has helped people around us take a good look at this. A few have told us that their views, their feelings about death have been altered. These people too have come to appreciate Anne for giving forth this announcement in such an exemplary way. And for that they are grateful and loving.*

Another part of the explanation of this presence of love is another belief I have, namely my belief in God. I believe that the Love, the God, is a powerful unseen force that helps bring it alive in the human creature.

CHAPTER 11

# The Importance of Pets

IN January of 2004, Kaira, our beloved black Lab died. Anne and I immediately decided that we needed to get another dog, "because one of us will probably die before the dog" and that dog will be very important to the one left. Truer words were never spoken.

In April we got a five-month-old puppy from the Prison Pet Partner Program at the Washington Women's Correctional Center here in Gig Harbor. The prison has a program for boarding, grooming and training of service dogs. We had boarded Kaira there since 1991. It is a wonderful program for the inmates as they receive training in caring for animals after leaving prison. But most of all, it gives the chosen women an opportunity to show their affection and receive affection from the dogs. As soon as Kaira died we contacted the PPPP, knowing that dogs given to them to be trained as service dogs sometimes flunk out. We said we would like to adopt such a dog. They called back and said they thought they had a dog we would like.

We took the dog for a short test period and found her perfect to our tastes: attentive, smart, house broken, obedient to basic commands and on a learning curve. We adopted the three-fourth black Lab and one-fourth Border collie and named her Daphne. We struggled with what to call her for several days. Then I thought of Greek mythology and of Daphne, the most beautiful of the nymphs pursued by Apollo. She escaped and was transformed into a most beautiful laurel tree. I somehow thought that the name Daphne fit our dog. Anne agreed.

Except for the narrowness of her face, her ease in sitting on command, and her enormous speed (I once clocked her running 21 miles an hour), she is like a Lab in all other respects. She is the most affectionate and snuggly dog I believe I have ever had.

Just seven months after we adopted Daphne we discovered the melanoma in Anne which took her life 10 months later. This dog has been a godsend for me!

When I come into the house bereft of Anne, there is a living energy that greets me in the presence of Daphne. How empty and forlorn this dwelling would be without her. She is constantly at my side except when she finds a place to spread out in the sun as it pours through a window or sliding glass door, or sitting at alert as she awaits the morning walk of the doe and her two fauns who traipse through the woods in our back yard. Daphne communicates her needs, which are mostly to be petted, to me patiently and easily.

Friends have commented how expressive her face is with her big brown eyes. I know instantly by looking into her eyes if she feels guilty, affectionate, ashamed, hungry or playful. Her need for exercise, fetching the ball, helps me keep to a daily routine of brisk walking and ball throwing. Without her I think I would not be so religious about taking my heart pumping walks up and down hills every day.

She is acute in spotting my feelings of sadness, excitement, tiredness, pain, and joy. She pulls off antics every day that make me laugh. We talk to each other quite a bit sometimes with just our eyes, other times with my voice.

She reminds me lovingly of my Anne by her enormous energy, willfulness, independence and sweet affection in caring for me.

I must relate how sensitive Daphne is. I wrote earlier in these pages about Anne and I saying our goodbyes and recording it on my iPod. I made a CD of the recording. It was about three months after Anne's death that I decided to listen to it.

I put the CD into my Mac in my upstairs office. Daphne was lying on the carpet at the head of the stairs right outside my office. My office has wood flooring. As I began to listen to the CD,

Daphne slowly arose, came into the office to lie on the floor next to me at the computer.

As I heard the CD for the first time, I cried at certain sections of it. When it ended, Daphne slowly arose and returned to her spot on the soft carpet at the head of the stairs. I looked down at the wood floor where she had been and saw a puddle of urine. I felt so sorry for her. Now, when I play the CD I make sure she is not in earshot.

Life would be quite empty without Daphne. I am blessed to have the health to care for her and have her. I have often wondered why more nursing homes do not have pets around so residents can express their affectionate side by petting and cuddling pets.

Anne and I were right – if one of us would die before the dog, the pet would be extremely important to whomever was left behind.

## Part II

# My Life After Anne

AFTER Anne died I continued on with my journaling. It is in the pages of my journal that the story of my life in grieving is recorded. Writing my journal is extremely helpful to me. It relieves the sharpness of painful feelings, brings me deeper into my soul and helps me make sense of life. In one entry I even wrote, "Journal, you are my best friend."

My life with Anne the 10 months she was moving to her certain death and these past four years of living without her have allowed me to have experiences that I could not have predicted, nor could ever imagined. I have benefited from being one with her for those 10 months and then being without her for four years.

In these chapters I describe some of my deepest thoughts, feelings, puzzles, struggles and experiences that I have never had before in my life.

In reading my experiences I hope that it will stir your imagination as to what might be the unique road you may have if you lose a loved one through death.

CHAPTER 12

# The Mystery of Sadness

I share my experience with sadness, what it offered to me and how I dealt with it in the following journal entries.

Journal - 25 days after Anne died on October 14, 2005

*"These moments of missing Anne, remembering Anne in so many different ways, always accompanied with the soft, sweet feeling of sadness, is fetching. It is almost addictive. I feel I could just stop my life and be eternally in these moments. My life of daily duties, pleasures, responsibilities is not as appealing as those moments of remembering and being with Anne.*

Journal - Four days later

*I came home last night after dinner. I was surprised at not feeling any loss of Anne, not feeling any sadness and loneliness. Anne was not on my mind. I was surprised at this because I thought I should be missing her.*

*What was going on? How could I not miss her – it was not even a month since her death. Was there something wrong with me? Was it due to the fact that yesterday my mind was consumed with the intricacies of the distribution of the trust and spending about three hours trying to get the cheapest airline ticket for my 12/10 trip?*

*Or was it that I had been in an "accepting of her death" mode for practically the entire past year? That Anne and I had looked death in the face and accepted it? Was it due to Anne's presence in my heart, healing me of the loss? There was a way I felt normal.*

*Could this experience of last night just be a temporary blip on the continuing line of grieving, mourning, and missing her?*

*I find myself feeling embarrassed right now as I write this, as if I shouldn't be feeling this way. Well, I'll just be open to what's next. For the first time I even thought about hitting a few golf balls.*

Journal - A year and 2 months later on January 9, 2007

*Every day I think of Anne in one way or another. Sometimes it triggers sadness and loneliness, other times not. Today, it seems for the first time, when I remembered her it was accompanied by a thought – "I can't believe she is dead".*

Journal - A year and six months after her death, June 20, 2007

*I just emptied a folder containing all the brochures of Anne and me doing workshops together – trying to make space in my file drawer.*

*I looked at these descriptions and pictures of us on the brochures going back to the late 80s. I felt the deepest sadness. The pain was as strong as it has ever been. And I thought my feelings of missing Anne, my sadness, my emptiness, my pain – was diminishing after 20 months of grieving. But just now, the pain was so deep – coming from just looking especially at one picture of young Anne and me - Anne still with her long hair, a turn on for me!*

*Will I ever get over my loss? Will this sadness, emptiness, gut pain ever lessen? This sudden unexpected shot of pain just made me want to give up, turn in my earthly life for whatever is next, hopefully to be with Anne somehow. It zapped my energy.*

*I just had to stop everything and write this. If the past teaches me, I know shortly that my "busy desk", my responsibility toward unfinished business, my caring for Daphne, will distract me from this agony now present in my body. Oh Anne, I miss you so!*

## Journal - Sunday, 2 years and 7 days after Anne died

*A thought came to me just now that had a flavor of newness to it, be it a deeper conviction or perhaps even a new thought entirely.*

*The thought – life is never going to be as great as it was with Anne. That's the reality. <u>Accept it</u>. The accepting of this reality had a "freeing" feeling attached to it. Somehow I felt stronger.*

*"Accept it" had a new power, force. I felt it deeper than ever before since Anne died. Could it be that it has just taken these two years of living in all the experiences I've had before I could experience this "accepting" in such a strong way?*

*I'll see what emerges.*

As I wrote earlier, the very writing of my Journal eased the sharpness of my sadness, allowed me to question the experience and find the goodness in it. It helped me to live with it. In the very writing, I was expressing the feeling rather than suppressing or distracting myself from it. I am a firm believer in feeling the emotion to gain from it and to find relief from it. We are wired to feel emotions. They are part of us for a good purpose. Remember my experience in the chapter "The Shock of Death". I just let myself freely cry and after about 15 minutes it ended. I had no need to continue – it had served its purpose.

CHAPTER 13

# My Search for Meaning

**JOURNAL** – Eight days after Anne died on October 14, 2005

*I'm going through Anne's papers, folders, and desk to put some order out of her scattered piles of stuff. Throwing away so many sheets of paper, cards, notes galore, feeling like part of me is leaving. I feel heavy and sad.*

*I wonder, after tidying up her affairs, will I have any meaning to live?*

WHEN in college I read a book that greatly influenced me, <u>Seven Storey Mountain</u> by Thomas Merton, a Trappist monk. I became very serious about pursuing a spiritual life and following the example of Jesus in living. I saw Jesus as the most striking person in human history in terms of how we should live. (I must immediately state that one of my journal entries is titled "The Confessions of a Failed Christian" for I admit I have not followed the example of Jesus with sufficient degree of fortitude.)

Later in the 60's I read another influential book, <u>Man's Search For Meaning</u> by Viktor Frankl, a psychiatrist who spent three years in Auschwitz Concentration Camp. He relates that those who lost meaning in their lives would quickly die from the cruelty of the Camp; those who had a strong meaning to live, did so. I saw that I had by then formed a strong meaning in my life, namely to pursue a spiritual life and to have Jesus as my model in life.

My early Catholic upbringing and living with my Grandmother

from 10-13 years of age had much to do with my later meaning in life. Grandmother was not a pious woman; she was a saintly woman. Her whole body and face bore the stature of a wise, earthy, peaceful, calm, loving and accepting person. As I reflect on life with Grandmother I realize she provided an environment that unconsciously conveyed the importance of the spiritual.

My readings allowed me to understand that Jesus placed loving others as primary, even in loving one's enemies (laying the groundwork for my later pacifism). In this loving I should feed the hungry, clothe the naked, care for the sick and the underprivileged. Jesus afflicted the comfortable and comforted the afflicted.

So my meaning in life took shape – to love, to make the world more just and peaceful. No wonder I participated in the civil rights and peace movements in the 60's and 70's. My meaning in life increased after I married Anne. Here was one person with whom I could pour out my love and over the years I experienced a loving as I had never before in my life. It was a loving and being loved that was transformational for me.

When Anne died, the object of my love vanished from me. My daily loving of Anne, my daily meaning in life was gone.

No wonder searching for meaning is a frequent topic in my journal.

## Journal – Three months into my life after Anne, January 16, 2006

*The question before my mind at this very moment is that to live, I must have a purpose, a purpose to energize me, to make my life worthwhile. What is this purpose?*

*I can't find it within me. I can intellectually make one up but that is just "thinking" of a purpose, trying to establish one out of my mind. But if I do that, from past experience, it just stays in the head and doesn't sink through into my heart, my soul, into the cells of my body. It doesn't become me.*

*Early on, my purpose was to change the world by making social structures just and fair and in doing that I would be following Jesus. I saw early on it wasn't sufficient just to give bread to the poor, as good as that is in itself, but the structures needed to change so that the poor have a chance to get a job with a living wage so with dignity they could feed themselves.*

*After marriage my purpose was to make the marriage as good as possible. In so doing, I fell more and more in love with Anne. Now I had two meanings – loving Anne and serving the world.*

*Now the object of my person-to-person love is gone. That person standing before me beckoned my very love. And toward the end I felt a pure love; my ego seemed to vanish.*

*Add to that, having no blood offspring of my own, I feel I am not really needed by anyone. In living with Anne we needed each other. We needed each other for fun, companionship, absolute intimacy of soul and body. We became one. We needed each other in whom to trust the depth of our thoughts and soul. We needed each other to be free - free to share all, free to expand ourselves, free to grow in love and trust and loyalty. We knew that we needed the other to be there for us. That is a life! That is a life worth living!*

*Now what is left to live for?*

### Journal - Six months later, April 21, 2006

*...This afternoon something powerful hit me. It wasn't new, but it had receded in my memory. I felt an excitement that stirred up energy in my body. I felt <u>creative!</u> ...*

*Could this be the answer to my malaise? My meaning in life is to be creative in some way?*

### Journal - Two months later, June 9, 2006

*...I wonder if this thought may have something to do with my searching for meaning?*

*Since I have been living my life of loss and grieving*

*I have become so much more sensitive, compassionate, empathetic to others who are going through losses including death. For years I've guided people through loss as a family therapist, but never have I <u>felt</u> the anguish of others as I can now.*

*My experience in this last year and a half has so tenderized me, that I even notice myself engaging with all other people now in a new, slower, more feeling, more time giving, more patient looking into their eyes than ever before. Along with that I find myself less judgmental and willing to let others have their views so oppositional to mine and accept them with their beliefs as theirs.*

*Being with others in the moment at hand is totally sufficient. If the next moment never comes, it is okay. That is, if I die in the present moment of full engagement and there is no next moment or next thing to do, that's perfectly okay.*

## Journal - A year after Anne's death, October 13, 2006.

*Perhaps it's good for me to feel this restless, lost, somewhat meaningless life. I would like to listen to my insides to get some answers. But perhaps being answerless is good for me. Being without answer has a feeling of vulnerability which reminds me that indeed everything is vulnerable – me, my world, the world. It could all blow up; I could just keel over dead.*

*To live in the moment.*

## Journal - About a month later

*Apparently I can't live fully engaged in each moment or perhaps I need something more than that as my anguish in finding meaning grows.*

*Again this morning I am aware of the near mechanical motions of my living. Going through the steps of arising from sleep, dressing, taking the dog out, getting the Sunday paper, fixing the coffee, breakfast and then reading the paper.* Each action has some slight pleasure, satisfaction to it, but in the long run, in the larger picture of my life, what's it all about?

Even though as I write this I can see some good that I do – keeping in touch with Anne's boys and families – yet it doesn't ever seem enough. Even the prospect of teaching in UK later this month, planning an early arrival in London to see some plays – seems to have more feeling of drag than excitement.

It is hard to live in the here and now when the here and now lacks some deep purpose. My healthy body keeps life somewhat pleasant. But I often think, what if I got sick, lost energy and desire, felt miserable – would I simply give up wanting to live? It seems that you have got to live for something; you just can't live just to live. Living for the sake of living is not a sufficient reason to live. Living has to be for some higher purpose. I don't think I would be feeling this way if I had not been married to Anne, had not been so much in love with her.

If I had not that experience, I think I would have been excited and happy in "changing the world' which had given meaning to my life prior to Anne.

But having tasted what life was like with Anne, having tasted the thrill of loving her so totally, nothing else compares to that. Compared to that love, all is straw. As hard as I now try to generate meaning, purpose, excitement, drive, and vision of a future, as hard as I try – I can't do it. It isn't a given either. God is not giving it to me, nor is any other agency. Nor should I expect it to be given to me. I should gain it for myself.

But I can't find it. How long will this go on like this?

I hear myself utter a deep sigh.

Journal - December 10, 2007 Two years, two months after Anne. Note it is a year before I write anymore about searching for meaning, even though prior to that I have many Journal entries about this issue.

> *My journaling reflects how often I search for meaning in my life. Why this struggle? Living with Anne I had a multi-meaning life. I was engaged in various activities, some strictly pleasure, others to better the world and the human condition. But these activities were energized also through my living with Anne and her almost invisible support and congruence with these activities. Also in living with Anne, we were mutually, always <u>stimulating</u> each other just by our presence and liveliness. We so enjoyed each other's sparking one another whether it was through lightness, humor and laughter or through deep reflections and discussions or by playing together and beneath it all was our love for each other. Our mutual trust of each other allowed for our being free – free to be totally ourselves emotionally, intellectually, affectionately and spiritually.*
>
> *All this invigorated our living and we just naturally, almost unconsciously did things that meant much to us. Our life was a life full of meaning – a meaning of being and acting.*
>
> *So when Anne died, this constant sparking of each other vanished. The vacuum was so large. My emptiness feels like a meaningless existence.*
>
> *This is a distressful awakening.*
>
> *I wonder what will happen next.*

During the Spring of 2008 I find that my angst in searching for meaning is far less. It seems that I am more calmly seeking it, awaiting for it to appear as it were. I feel more content in trying to enjoy each moment while also welcoming any emptiness I feel as an invitation to go deeper into myself to see what might be there. I think that this may be due to the lessening of the frequency of feeling lonely and sad.

CHAPTER 14

# The Disappearance of God

FOR the first time in my life my firm belief in God began to weaken. It wasn't that I had any beef with God, but God just became unimportant to me during the 10 months of Anne's dying.

That unimportance continued after her death. Then one day I had what I call my first agnostic experience; it was very empowering. I began to rethink how my faith in God developed and the nature of "faith" itself.

The following selections from my Journal describe this journey away from God and perhaps into a deeper faith, which may be something different than I had ever experienced before.

Journal October 7, 2005 Seven days <u>before</u> Anne died

*What explains what happened inside me last night? It seemed like a sudden eruption of my mindset. It was like a new thought paradigm. I was afraid, and am still afraid to say it, to write it. It was like - it doesn't make any difference if there is a God or not – at least as far as living is concerned. If there is no God then my previous psychological, spiritual structure is suddenly changed. My own language and way of viewing life is changed.*

*What brought this on? Was I angry? Was I anxious or selfish? Was I peeved? Resentful? Was I afraid? Or was I evolving? Was I moving into a new wisdom, a new clarity, a new simplicity?*

*I do know that for the past several years I have moved*

*further and further away from "religion," religious practices and the institutions of religion.*

*Last night, one of Anne's friends recommended to me to help Anne fantasize "going up the mountain to God." I couldn't do it for her. All I told Anne is "I only know two things for sure; one is that you are dying, and two is that you have lived a life of great achievement and joy as well as sorrow. Your children, all the people you have helped, your efforts to make the world better – for this you can be filled with gratitude and satisfaction. This is the imagery I can offer you, to think of all you've done, all the love in your heart, and feel all the gratitude and happiness in your heart." She could do that and did feel peace and a quiet joy.*

*I couldn't imagine her going up a mountain. It might have worked for her if I believed it would help. But it's like I didn't believe in it. I could only offer what I believed in.*

Journal - November 1, 2005, Just 19 days after Anne died, I wrote the following.

*A man of faith says, "God, what do you want of me now? What meaning do you want from me?" To put it differently – God is giving me life, health, therefore God wants me to live, therefore I must find some purpose to my life so I don't waste what's left, so I don't betray the Giver of life.*

*A man of no faith says, " I can choose to live or not to live; I have no obligation to something called God – it is fully my decision". So, if I decide to live I must find a purpose for it, a meaning for my living. However this decision to live or not to live is not totally dependent upon me alone. This decision is heavily influenced by my love, attachment, gratitude, and loyalty to my beloved Anne – who loved life with gusto every moment she had <u>to feel alive</u>.*

*Till I reach that bodily state of dying I will live as fully as I can. Know what, the "man of no faith" has more determination to live than the "man of faith". <u>It was a strange</u>*

*feeling – as soon as I wrote the "man of no faith…" I felt a greater power in me!!*

Later, about 30 minutes, I thought about why was it stronger? What came to me is that as the "man of faith" I was somehow dependent on God, like a grown child can still be dependent on a parent. I was in God's hand. God was still leading me like a parent leads the child. As a man of no faith I felt more adult, like it was my decision, not God's. It was up to me to decide on my own, not beholden to do what God wanted. That's why I think I felt stronger, more powerful as the "man of no faith". Ah, could not this be the essential meaning of God becoming a man. Man is equal in some way to God, not in an arrogant sort of way, but as being fully in charge of his life as an adult should be. Depend on God, well, what about that? Maybe that's not such a good thing after all.

This is a new thought for me in my 79 years of being. I often wondered what might be the strength of being an atheist or agnostic. Could it not be like the adolescent who really leaves home and ceases to be "dependent" upon the more powerful parent? The adolescent becomes an "atheist" in relation to the parent – as if the parent does not exist! And thus the adolescent must become independent and take charge of one's own life and living. Once achieved, then the grown son or daughter can face the fact that the parent is there, but is not as parent as much as just a person much like the grown daughter or son.

## Journal - Two months after Anne's death, December 14, 2005

I've become aware of a growing preoccupation with - "Is there really a God?" Or "Do I really believe in God?" Anne always said that I believed more than she. I think that what is making me think this way is that during that last ten months of Anne's accepting death and then so obviously seeing her daily shutting down toward the end, made *me totally focused, preoccupied, on Anne. My love for her became as total as never before. It seemed to take on a purity of love, stripped of all self-interest.*

*In that total giving to Anne I had few if any thoughts of God. God receded from my mind and spirit. God was not important; Anne was. I don't think I once prayed a prayer of petition. Never did I blame God. I never asked God to save Anne. I never asked God to relieve her of pain. The meds were doing that job. God simply was unimportant to me. God receded, or I from God.*

*Then it occurred to me, could it be that in totally loving Anne I was loving God too. If there were a God, God would be in Anne. I didn't need to distinguish between the two. It was like I, in caring for Anne in her dying process, did not really need God as a separate reality. I wonder, did Anne need God or feel a need for God? I have no evidence of that. Perhaps it was just a given.*

*When I considered - "you ought to think of God," pray – it seemed inappropriate. It was a weird, strange ten months of living with Anne and not the "God" figure. Perhaps the God-in-Anne was the reality – in loving Anne I was in touch with God without the name God coming into play – or the reality of God.*

Could God simply be the energy of loving?

## Journal - Six months after Anne's death, April 23, 2006

*Since Anne's death I have had moments of wavering from my firm belief in God, to that of being agnostic. But amazingly those agnostic moments did not bother me. I was quite content to live with either outcome – God – or no God – death final or death a transition. I felt secure with either possibility. I didn't have to believe for my own comfort and well-being. My grandparents and parents were either up there pulling strings or not. I feel okay with either.*

*I think these agnostic moments have purified me of "needing to believe for my own comfort". I think that I have moved into a more pure state of simple trust. All I have is the present moment and do the best I can with it. That is sufficient.*

*Anne may be with my spirit or may not be. Okay I feel a tinge now, wouldn't it be nicer if she were? But then again, maybe not. Would I be freer if she weren't in my spirit? No that's not it – she's always said, after I am gone find another woman. I laughed and said, "no way, unless you pick her before you die." And it is still inconceivable to me to ever relate to another person with the kind of love I had with Anne. I almost feel it wouldn't be fair to the other woman.*

*But is this not living in past memories? Does this not enslave me to some degree? I am the result of my past and cherish all of it for what it has meant to me in maturing me. So that part is still in me even though my perception of it has changed so that I can honor it and live more fully in the present moment with that past.*

*So now I must begin to think of the past with Anne so as not to live in that past but to honor it in such a way that it simply allows me to live more fully in the present moment, in the here and now.*

*Perhaps the key is to be agnostic about whether or not Anne is indeed in my spirit at this moment. If so, okay; if not, okay. But I do feel that I would like for her to be in my spirit now too, to love me and be loved. Life perhaps is only in the present moment. That is one way eternity is defined, - the Eternal Now.*

If God were one with Jesus, could not God be one with Anne, so in loving Anne I am loving God without having to distinguish between Anne and God?

Journal - About a year after the last entry above, June 10, 2007

*As I awoke this morning the thought occurred to me – why do Catholics go to Mass?*

*Although I am sure the complete answer is far more complex than my little answer. The Catholic religion has clear answers to such things as – is there a God, what kind of a God is God, is there an afterlife, what is the moral code that should govern our lives, what is the purpose of life? These clear answers leave little or no uncertainty. They answer some very basic life questions with certitude and in believing one has certitude about one's life.*

*This certitude makes one feel very secure. There is no doubt about the future life of eternal happiness if one lives up to God's commands. In the midst of failing health, being increasingly weak and vulnerable, one feels secure in one's faith, in the certitude of answers to "what will happen to me."*

*Part of this security is believing that one is in the hands of God – the all powerful and loving God who will take care of "me, no matter what." I am basically weak; God will take care of me. And what greater feeling is there than to feel safe and secure?*

*A Catholic's religion gives a clear framework in which to live life. In this world of turbulence, uncertainty, fear, this religion offers security and safety even as one dies.*

*No wonder mankind has apparently, from what we know of history, taken on religion, taken on believing in God or gods who direct our lives into happiness, even if it takes place after death.*

*Living my life now, alone without Anne and all the support we gave to each other; feeling my aging as never before with the attendant vulnerabilities; worrying about what will happen to me as I lose the ability to live independently, - scares me to some degree.*

*Yet there is something in me that rejects the notion that "just put yourself in God's hands and all will be well". It seems to me like a copout, a refusing to take responsibility for my life, my future, my own feeling of being scared and insecure.*

*What is better for me, for my human development till I die – to feel safe or to feel unsafe? To feel certain or to feel uncertain?*

*Is it better to assume the fullest amount of responsibility for one's life, direction, or to relax that a bit and throw myself into the hands of God?*

*Is it better for me to believe in the loving God, to put myself into God's hands? Or is it better to trust in self and others here on earth? <u>Trust in being okay with feeling unsafe</u>, insecure? To trust that it is all right to feel vulnerable, dependent, weak, dying? To trust that, if there is a God, this God would want me to assume as much responsibility as I can for my life, diminishment and death?*

*What is better?*

## Journal July 2, 2007

*It's three months short of two years since Anne died. The summer evenings in the NW are so splendid, so beautiful, so peaceful – cool and soft, birds singing everywhere in the midst of the forest we live in.*

*After dinner c. 7:30 p.m., I just had to go out. I took Daphne with me. First we took a ride to explore new territory out in the country. The trees are so magnificent. It's pleasantly cool this evening. The day was in the 70s.*

*I will never end exploring all the territory even within 10 miles radius from where I live. Daphne was alert, watching till we turned for home to hit familiar streets, and then she slumped into the seat with her head between her front paws.*

*Once home, we took a short walk. Again the memories of these NW, cool summer evenings with Anne returned. My excursions now are only half joyful without her.*

*As I write this at 8:15 p.m., the trees surrounding the house are cutting down the evening light sky. Sunset is upon* us. *As I write, the birds have not retired yet; their symphony still continues. Ah, I hear a firecracker in the distance. The 4th is two days away. How I wish Anne were with me enjoying this peaceful, beautiful, quiet evening. Could Heaven be any greater than this? Only if I were with Anne – then this would be Heaven on earth. Without Anne, it lacks something. Something is missing. I don't feel complete.*

*My love, I love you! Where are you? Do you exist? Only if you could speak to me, visit me. But no, there is something wrong with that. Death was part of your journey; disappearance from bodily form was your destiny – as it is for all of us one day.*

*It's funny, before you died, I firmly believed in Heaven, an afterlife. Now for some unexplained reason I fear to hold that belief. Why?*

*If I held on to it, it might be only to be consoled. But then would my "faith" be only a make-believe "faith" so as to be consoled?*

*Without this "faith" I have not that consolation. Is it not better to be in a dark night of the unknown, "not so sure"? To suffer, not knowing, not believing – leaves me to rely only in some sort of <u>naked trust</u>. Yes, what is left is to trust in the unknown. To trust the mystery I live in. Yes, it is a naked trust in nothingness. To trust that there is a heaven, an afterlife, a God is consoling but now I suspect such consolation. Such consolation could make a believer out of me. So it would not be God who makes a believer out of me.*

*Is this not some sort of the dark night of the soul I'm tentatively entering? I hope what I'm experiencing is a true path <u>– but the uncertainty of the path may be the essence of the path.</u> It's like I have to face it.*

## Journal September 27, 2007 Almost two years since Anne died

*If there is nothing after death, it does seem strange that we grow so loving, so wise, so mature - only to die and go totally out of existence.*

*As I write this I can't help but believe that our love for and with each other introduced a certain energy of love in the universe that was one small contribution to the betterment of those who come after us. Yes, we still live in a world of violence, a world that accepts the need of a military, of wars, of killing and maiming to protect the "interests" of the good people who possess the might. But perhaps more people than ever before are coming to understand that war, killing is not the answer – but loving of the "enemy" is the answer. Perhaps the love energy generated from the time of Jesus is having its beneficial effect. Perhaps more people now agree with Jesus and that he wasn't some wild-eyed, impractical visionary on some dumb quixotic adventure. Instead perhaps people are beginning to see that Jesus was the most hardheaded, practical person of all.*

*If there is an afterlife of a heavenly type of existence – well and good, hallelujah! But if there isn't, suffice it that all people who lose themselves in loving others are electrifying the universe with the energy of love so that our children and grandchildren will have a more lovable existence than we.*

## Journal December 8, 2007 Two years and two months after Anne

*I've been tossing and turning; wide awake and thinking. Thinking about God, about Anne, about my living in 2005 the year of Anne's dying, living in 2006 and 2007.*

*"I believe in God, the Father Almighty, Creator of Heaven and Earth and all things visible and invisible" – the opening words of the Catholic Creed. But what does that really mean?*

*In reading the Old Testament I could also say I believe in God, the destroyer of mankind except for Noah and his family; or I believe in God the Warrior who told the Israelites to kill all the people in Canaan. Moving to the New Testament I could say I believe that God became incarnate in Jesus who said love the enemy, do good to those that harm you. What a switch for this God I believe in. Or do I believe in a God who both gives commands to kill and to love the enemy?*

*"Believe in God," - to believe is to hold on to something as true without any proof for it. If it could be proved you wouldn't have to believe; you would know it.*

*The word "God" has a meaning. God is He, or is it She or It? What, who is the God that I believe in?" God is a noun so the word "God" has a meaning and being a noun God is an "It" or a subject that is put in front of a verb that does something. God is a Creator of all things visible and invisible.*

*A word is an expression of a meaning that emanates from our intelligence. Animals by and large don't speak in words. Humans do and we have thick dictionaries of thousands of words – each word symbolizing a meaning of some sort. "Father, Mother" are begetters of human life.*

*And all these meanings symbolized by words are an attempt to label what we experience in our finite world. In the 20$^{th}$ century a new reality appeared – a machine that could do new things. We had to find a new word to symbolize this new creation and so we designed the noun "computer."*

*And so humans long ago experienced the earth and fish and animals and sky and sun and they couldn't figure where it all started, so they came up with a new word, "God." - God the Creator. Gradually the word took on other meanings such as omnipotent, omniscient, omnipresent.*

*So what is it that I really believe when I say, "I believe in God?" Do I not really mean that I don't know what the origin of the world is so I say I believe in something that I just call God? As I create things with my hands and out of wood comes a statue, so someone must have made the earth – it's the only experience I know of. So do I just believe in the conclusion to a line of reasoning within me? I believe in a conclusion that long ago my ancestors thought of.*

*But wait, perhaps some humans experienced something that spoke to them from out of the blue. "I am God, your maker. Do what I tell you and I will reward you. If not, I will punish you." Perhaps the word God, Yahweh, Allah came from some sort of human experience rather than from a rational process trying to figure out where this universe came from.*

*There are ancient writings testifying to this phenomenon. Moses came down from the mountain and told the people that God appeared to him and he wrote down God's commandments on stone. Later others, called prophets, claimed that God spoke to them. In other words, some individuals had an experience and they called it God. They might have named the experience "Awesome," or "Presence" or an overwhelming "Power." Or perhaps they could have called it an "Experience beyond any words". The people believed what Moses and the Prophets said. The people believe what Joseph Smith, the teenager said.*

*My personal "belief in God" most likely began when my parents told me to say my prayers to this invisible, silent thing they referred to as God. So I began to believe in God. Then there were the statues, pictures of holy ones who believed in God; then came the nuns, priests, other family members who all believed in God and taught me specific qualities of this God – God knows all, is everywhere, is all powerful, made all and has prepared a Heaven and Hell for us depending on how we live. So I came to believe in God.*

*But am I believing in God or believing in my parents, relatives, and teachers? I believed in these people! I trusted these authority figures. And these people told me that long time ago God appeared to some select people who told others of their exalted experience. So these people simply believed in what a few of their fellow humans told them! So is it faith in people or faith in God?*

*I don't think I've had an experience of God. I've had an extraordinary body experience or a Zen experience of being totally in the here and now a few times, but that is it. I've had an experience of loving Anne that is hard to describe, and it was a new kind of experience for me. But I am now very reluctant to call it an experience of God. Some say to me, "that was an experience of God." But how do they know? Why do they call it "God?" Why not just say that it is a glorious human experience that anyone might have given the right place and circumstances.*

*Perhaps my extraordinary love experience of Anne during the 10 months before she died was an indication or a pointing to the reality of a loving beyond us. Perhaps an indication of the mystery that we all live in, a mystery so profound that someday here or after life we will experience it as that of what we label "God." I don't know.*

*I am open to it though. Perhaps death may be the greatest entry into the "whatever" experience.*

*Oh death, happy entrance to that I don't know, I welcome you when it is time. In the meanwhile I'll return to my apprenticeship in "loving," simply trusting in whatever comes my way. It is now 2:10 a.m.*

I think that these experiences described in my Journal have something to do with the benefits of my grieving. I think that I have never gone as deeply into my inner-self as I have these last two and half years.

So far, the conclusion of my experience in the disappearance of God is that I am at peace. I am at peace in simply <u>trusting</u>. I trust, in some strange way, the mystery of life, the mystery of the love Anne and I had for each other, the mystery of the vast unknown I live in. Also the vast interconnectedness of nature somehow gives me some evidence to trust. It is in trusting the unknown, even not knowing whether there is a God or not, that I find peace.

Ironically, the word "faith" comes from the Latin "fides." In Cassell's Latin English Dictionary the first two meanings of "fides" are "trust" and "confidence."

CHAPTER 15

# Living in Mystery

SOON after Anne died I found myself facing the unknown in life. About a year after Anne died I reflected more about this phenomenon. I began to think that I live more in the unknown than in the known. Life seemed more uncertain than certain. I express this development in a few entries of my Journal beginning about a year after Anne died

Journal September 27, 2006

*Why am I feeling so sad and tender right now...*

*Now I realize that under everything there is only mystery. Mystery, the unknown, is what seems fundamental – root – the foundation of all above it such as all we experience as real, - what we see, hear, touch and think. Are these bits of consciousness only a façade? The basic reality is mystery. Mystery to accept and embrace, be at peace with. Mystery, the invisible, unproven, untouchable reality. Now I am feeling humble in the face of mystery.*

*Knowing that all is basically mystery doesn't really take faith to believe it. The evidence, the experience of mystery, of not knowing is too clear. What takes faith is to believe that in the end, all will be well. Ah, now I experience in me that mystery takes on sort of a loving feeling. I believe that the mystery, the unknown is a loving sort of mystery of some kind – that makes me feel safe.*

*So this is the gift of the sadness I can't fathom at this moment – it leads me to the foundation of all – mystery, unknown.*

*Alas, I feel better.*

## Journal - A year and four months without Anne, February 14, 2007

*I can't believe it. I just opened up an album on one of my bookshelves, looking for a file. I didn't know what was in it, as I hadn't looked at it for years. In this album I find a valentine card Anne gave to me early in our marriage. It amazes me that on this Valentine's Day 2007, I would just happen to look at this album after all these years! What explains these kinds of coincidences? Life, creation is such a mystery.*

*Since December of 2004 I have grown more and more to recognize and live within the uncertainty of mystery. Such living lacks a feeling of being in control. It forces me to trust, know it's OK not to be in control, be open to surprises, live more fully in the present, here and now, and be open to whatever.*

## Journal - A month later, March 6, 2007

*Just before taking up the pen to write this morning, the questions arise again in my mind – why do I often think about questions such as –*

*Why am I blessed with so much health at 81?*
*What is my meaning to live these days after Anne?*
*Why do I not find a driving force in my life?*
*What sense do I make out of my life without Anne?*
*Is that zest in living I had with Anne due to my love for Anne, our loving and fun companionship, never to be mine again?*
*Am I to live a half zestful life till I finally die?*

> *These questions keep reappearing even though in this journal at times I find answers to them. But the answers fade away into nothing and I am stuck with the same questions.*
>
> *There is a sneaky part of me that begins to see that I like these questions. They make me feel deeper, more spiritual – even more loving in some indescribable way. These questions demand my deeper self to come alive.*
>
> *These questions speak to the mystery of myself, to the mystery of love, to a life absent of a loved one. Life with Anne was a constant living answer to these unspoken questions. The answer given in living the love with Anne made the questions remain unconscious or perhaps nonexistent. I had the answer provided in my very living so I was never aware of the questions begging for an answer as now. But now the questions surface in my consciousness and make me aware of the power of love between two people, the power of the mystery all life is. Is it better now to have questions rather than answers? The former awakens the depth of mystery, the unanswerable in all of life; the latter made life zestful. Could living in mystery now make mystery the God?*

## Journal - A year and half after Anne died, April 26, 2007

> *In reading pages 202-207 (<u>From Certainty to Uncertainty; The Story of Science</u> by Francis David Peat) I have somewhat of an understanding of my feeling lost at times; not knowing what to do, filled with questions about my life; on a deeper level not knowing who I really am. I find myself an enlarging mystery. At any given moment am I really the person, the actor strutting on this stage of life that I think I am? Do others see me differently than I see myself? But the deeper question is, - is the way I perceive myself the real me? Is my self-perception a delusion? Or part delusion? I want to not only be true to myself, I also*

want to <u>be</u> my true self. I don't want to walk through life kidding myself as to who I am and what I am.

After pages 202-207 I have a slightly different take on the above questions. This small section suggests that we can never get a fix on ourselves because we are never "fixed", i.e. I am not a stable thing, a stable "I." I am always in process, always changing from moment to moment. My essence is fluidity not fixed. However I live in a world of apparent stable, fixed things, called reality. This desk I'm writing on is fixed – it is not apparently changing from moment to moment. So it is easy to think that reality is somewhat fixed. Whereas the suggestion of pages 202-207 is that I am essentially always in motion, always changing so that the person, the "I" I was yesterday is not the person I am today. The "I" who just wrote the last sentence is not the "I" writing this sentence. We know that each moment of breath, of thinking changes the brain, and over time in some way changes my genes.

So no wonder I get confused and lost in trying to figure me out. The "who I am" that I knew five years ago is not the "who I am" today. That is clear.

So in these moments of "feeling lost", of worrying that I am not in touch with my real self and therefore live in a delusion – are moments that have some normality to them. These are moments that I should not worry too much about. Just try to be as honest with myself and my feelings as I can be, knowing that at any given time I will never know the complete, the total, real me. I can only get as much of an honest awareness of me as I learn to be self-aware from moment to moment. <u>That's all I can do.</u>

## Journal - A month later, May 16, 2007

I see so clearly as never before that I am in a great transition in my life. My experience of what seems to be real is that of existing in mystery more than in reality.

*More and more my "truth", if even that is the appropriated word, is that the only thing I know is my own experience at any given moment. When I read books, articles, I seem to agree or disagree, I seem to understand most of the time what I am reading – but there is an eerie feeling about reading and talking ideas. They don't stick to the ribs like my own personal experiences and thoughts, feelings, actions – as exemplified in my journaling.*

*I am aware of how much I am unaware. I know how much I don't know especially about me. The old bromide about "know thyself" is good as a goal, but my experience is telling me that I know very little about me in spite of thinking I do; and that much of what I think I know about me is very distorted. More and more, I have come to accept this and accept that I simply live in more mystery than not, and <u>that is okay</u>. Naturally, I would like to be more in touch consciously with who I am and what I am; but I feel greater peace in letting go of needing to know about me. However, I still pursue self-knowledge as it has many benefits, and it is also fun and exciting to probe mysteries.*

I think living alone, the depth of feelings I've had since Anne's death, and expressing myself in my Journal have contributed to my experiencing the reality of mystery. I think I experience this sense of living in mystery more deeply than at any other time in my life. I am happy that I am at peace with not knowing. It has awakened some sort of an ability to surrender to "not knowing." I feel that I can trust this mystery. Sometimes I experience it as a benign, living reality. It is a peaceful experience.

## Chapter 16

## Three Important Dreams

**I**N my education and training as a family therapist I learned how dreams are our friends, even horrible dreams. I also agree with the school of thought that only the dreamer can accurately interpret one's dreams.

Since Anne's death I have had three dreams that I deem most important to me. I share excerpts from my Journal entries about each of them.

Journal October 14, 2006 - Exactly one year after Anne died

*I don't know whether I was asleep and it was a dream, or that I was semi-awake and it just came to me, or whether I was awake and I created the picture, the thought. But however it was, there I was reliving the scene in the hospice room of Anne's last breath. It seemed as vivid as the real scene. Yet the strong emotions of crying and disbelief were absent in the dream this morning. When I awoke I was aware of the feeling in the dream; it was a feeling of calm peace. Then it dawned on me this is the first year anniversary of Anne's death! In these past 12 months, never once have I had a dream of Anne!*

*I got up and went to the bathroom, peed and then put in my contact lenses thinking about all this, the dream and my feelings. I don't know exactly why I felt at peace. Was it because I just felt good about having that dream come to me without my deliberately conjuring it up? Or did I feel good thinking that it was Anne contacting me through this medium?*

*There has been a way in which over this past year I have wanted to hear from Anne, to have Anne somehow contact me, to let me know she is okay and still present in some way more than just in my memory and heart.*

*I have written to her of late but never got an answer. I have uttered the words "Anne let me hear from you in some way" – all of this to no avail. Was I never to be contacted by her?*

*But this morning in the dream, after it was over, I did not feel sad, I just felt good – sort of at peace. And I don't precisely know why.*

*When Anne died I said to myself – no life changes for one year. I just continued on with my life, my involvements, pretty much as it was before Anne died – of course absent the caring for her in her final days. What was added to my life was doing all the things she did like cooking, thinking about what to eat, etc; also I lived with the sadness ever present of her being gone, the loneliness, the lack of "zest" in my life, the empty feeling of why live on?*

*I was living on automatic pilot; most of the time my daily activities seem to distract me consciously from my sadness and loneliness. And so I feel this way even now except the "emptiness of living" doesn't seem to be so present now at 6:37 a.m. Yet I do not feel that some other feeling, awareness has replaced the empty feeling of "why live on".*

*I just feel somewhat content in the "waking" state – waiting for what's next.*

*I think I prefer this explanation of my dream, i.e. as that of being contacted by Anne. That makes me feel good about Anne existing on some level and being okay, happy and at peace. Or am I just making this meaning up subconsciously to make myself feel good?*

*I don't know but for now I am content and even content about not knowing for sure why I feel content.*

> *Perhaps I feel content because by that dream I have not forgotten Anne at this one-year anniversary, who knows. May I continue just to feel a contented presence in my life.*

This dream was certainly my friend for it told me that there was change in me. I was not in shock at her death; I was not in such a heavy sadness. I was at peace; I accepted it. I felt relief.

The next dream took place about three months after the one described above. It was about my dog Daphne. The following entry explains itself.

## Journal January 25, 2007

> *I lay around in bed till about 8:30 a.m. since I had nothing to do, nothing to get up for. A series of short dreams flickered in and out of my semi-sleep. It is amazing how a dream can make so clear a reality that I don't see in my awaken life.*
>
> *The dream this morning was of my black lab, Daphne. She has a more slender and long body than most labs I have had. It may be due to her being one fourth Border Collie. Outside of that she looks every bit like a lab. She has a very expressive face and brown eyes that friends have commented on.*
>
> *One of her tender acts of affection is to sit before me while I am sitting. She slowly puts one paw up on my leg or lap, looking into my eyes for further permission, then her other paw, still looking for further permission. If my eyes say OK, she slowly rises on her back legs and softly puts her front legs around my neck in an embrace and licks my ears. I, of course, hug her in return.*
>
> *Well, my dream this morning was of Daphne doing this. But in the dream the affectionate feeling was heightened. Perhaps prior to the dream, I may have been feeling the sad loss of affectionate touching and embracing that Anne and I had in our life together. When I awoke I sharply felt*

*the need for affection in my life. I realized in a clearer, undistracted way the importance of affection in human life. I was so grateful that while I had no human with whom to share affection, I had this dog that is so affectionate and receives affection so gratefully.*

This dream was important to me in that it made very explicit to me just how important affection is in my life and that it is okay to deeply miss it and want it. Till this dream I think I had been avoiding seeing this so clearly and bluntly. Accepting this truth added to my wholeness and peace.

Journal - Two months later, March 12, 2007 - Monday 4:30 a.m.

*Saturday morning Marc called me with the news – Evan (his son just short of his 21st birthday) had died in a snowmobile accident; an avalanche took him down. It happened Friday afternoon in Canada on a mountain about six hours from Winthrop. I drove over yesterday, Sunday, arriving c. 4 p.m. with Daphne.*

*Went to bed at 9:30 p.m. after reading a bit. Awoke about 3:30 a.m. with this terrible dream. The feeling was one of being betrayed by my fellow workers – four of us were attorneys working to defend civil rights and bring about social justice. Behind my back the three of them decided to turn the practice entirely into serving Wall Street.*

*In the dream I felt this feeling of betrayal. I can't ever remember in my life having this deep, intense, absolutely awful feeling before. Betrayed.*

*I became furious – how could you do this – turn your backs from helping individuals, finding justice in this world, a better life in this world – and instead become servants, slaves to Wall Street, whose culture is to make money and possess power? Secretly in my head I thought of the new name for their firm, WSW, (WALL STREET WHORES). I ended the dream telling them to leave this firm and start their own WSW. They asked what that stood for. I told them that perhaps one day they might discover the answer.*

*This feeling of betrayal was absolutely the worst feeling I have ever had. Well, perhaps fear has been my worst feeling, but the feeling in the dream was awful. I can't ever remember feeling this intense feeling of betrayal.*

*Awake, I pondered – why this dream? Why this feeling? At 5 a.m., now, I still don't know for sure why.*

*As I lay in bed, awakened from this horrible dream, I pondered.*

*If any dream, it should have been a dream with the feeling of loss, loss of a loved one, loss of Evan. Yet this dream wasn't that.*

*Why this dream, at this time, at this place? Then it came to me...*

Over my years with Anne there was one aspect of her life that I had trouble understanding. There was an event in her life in which she felt betrayed. She lost considerable weight over it. I could never understand why such an event could be so devastating that it would cause such loss of weight. The betrayals in my life were small; they never produced such anguish and pain as I had in my dream.

The betrayal in my dream allowed me to understand what she went through. It put together some missing pieces in understanding Anne that were important to me. Anne would talk about trust and loyalty in such a way that it was obvious that they were extremely important to her. She was fierce about it. My dream let me understand more deeply how <u>trusting</u> is so basic to allowing oneself to love another. I now understand all people who feel deeply betrayed. This dream was a gift to me.

CHAPTER 17

# What To Do About Death

**ABOUT** eight months after Anne died, I began to think more about death and my own dying and how to prepare for it. My Journal reveals what an ongoing struggle this has been and how my thinking evolved.

The following two entries are concerned about death in general and about Jesus' death.

Why Not Thank God For Death

I had two thoughts about death I have never considered before. The first one is expressed in my Journal April 10, 2006, about six months after Anne's death.

> *I just had a new thought. We all thank God when a child is born, or when we recover from an illness based on the assumption that God has something to do with birth and recovery. But we don't seem to thank God for death even though it is assumed that God has something to do with that too. So is God good in the first two instances and bad in the last? And by inference, is death itself bad? Since it is a part of life, part of our nature, how is it bad? Perhaps it is only our perception. Perhaps we think it bad only because we suffer the loss of the one who dies. Perhaps that is why some get angry with God, as if God shouldn't do such a terrible thing as to cause death.*
>
> *Yes, I think that the only bad thing about death is that*

*we who are left behind are stricken with sadness of our personal loss. On the other hand perhaps we should rejoice in the person achieving one's final destination, which we call death. <u>For who knows what glory may transpire in the actual moment of dying?</u> Could it be the most splendid, glorious moment in that person's entire existence since birth? Then we shout for joy for Anne who has achieved that special oneness with the Good of All, the Beauty of All, the Music of All, the Love of All, the Peace and Joy of All - that some of us prefer to call God, Allah, and other nouns trying to designate this reality.*

The second thought is expressed in my Journal just four days later on Good Friday, April 14, 2006.

*Strange, I have never thought of this – why do we call the day of Jesus' death, "Good"? What was good about it? It was a horrible, bloody, choking-suffocating execution of a "criminal" upon a cross between two other criminals. Jesus was unjustly charged, unjustly sent to a death driven by the fear of some leading Jews and the spineless Roman governor.*

*And Jesus chose not to oppose this unholy action; he chose to accept his fate, to accept his death. He knew his preaching by both word and more by example was threatening the status quo. Jesus understood this full well. But he was not going to allay their fears by changing his message and life style. If it meant his death, so be it. He believed his way of love, forgiving the enemy, doing good to those who harm you – was the real solution to evil, fear and human violence.*

*By suffering violence in the cause of love, even a love of one's enemies, he would be taking one more step toward healing man's weakness. He believed in the power of love to eventually overcome hate and fear and violence even though it seemed to fly in the face of common sense.*

*Perhaps that's why we call this Friday of his bloody crucifixion "Good Friday". It was his ultimate act of love as expressed with his words from the cross "Father, forgive them, for they know not what they do." Then he was ready to stop breathing, to die – "Into thy hands I commend my spirit."*

*Did not Anne, in her 10 months of accepting her death with peace and grace accompanied by moments of fear and worry as she felt the cancer grow in her belly, finally come to the point of seeing, sensing God and commit her spirit into those hands also?*

*Her face was calm, at rest, no expression of anguish, as she simply stopped breathing. Her body in that bed was relaxed. My belief is that she moved on to a new oneness with Love.*

*As I write this I notice that the weather is cloudy and damp, melancholy, like my spirit is now. It is a fitting weather for the Good Friday of Jesus' death. Will Sunday be a resurrection of sun and brilliance? Doesn't really matter, for life here on earth is a permanent mixture of brightness and melancholy. And both are good for the soul. Melancholy sobers us down, makes us reflective, go slowly, letting the serious side of our spirit come alive. Brightness speaks to us of energy, robustness, hope, smiles and beauty. One without the other only cripples us, leaves us only half alive. Sadness and laughter go together to make us whole. Laughter without sadness makes us silly. And sadness without laughter makes us boring and too heavy.*

*I enjoy my sadness in thinking of Anne, thinking of Anne not here in body, not with me with her energy, laughter, sharpness at times, facing life head on. I don't know, I guess I just appreciate her more than ever. Yes, her absence allows me to appreciate her all the more.*

*As I reread this now, I feel her in me, my silent, unobtrusive companion, helping me along in life, but in this different way. Or is it that I just want to feel her in me? It doesn't matter, whatever is, is.*

The following entries show how my thinking evolved about Anne's death and my own death,

### Journal - Eight months after Anne's death on June 10, 2006

*I awoke early this morning @ 5 a.m. A stream of thoughts went through my mind.*

*As our dog, Kaira, was so old, weak and in pain we were going to put her down; but before we could do that she had a seizure that put her down. Why is it that we feel it is humane to end a dog's life when that life is decrepit, filled with pain and no longer enjoyable? Yet with humans we let nature take its course. Anne couldn't get to the point to actively end her life even though for several weeks she said repeatedly she wanted to die.*

Why was Anne hesitant to end her life? Was she reluctant to end her life sooner due to the culture we were raised in? She wanted to die, but felt she should do nothing to hasten it except to will it to happen.

### Journal - ten months later teaching in Germany, 4:20 a.m., April 24, 2007

*If Anne had said to me 4 weeks before she died, "Bill, I'm no longer able to care for myself; my life is no longer enjoyable for me; I want to die. So tonight I want to bring my life here to a close. I am going to stop eating and drinking." If she would have said that to me I would have felt deep sadness due to my loss, but I would respect and honor her and would have helped her do what she wanted. I would have admired her courage and freedom.*

*As it was, I think her religious background kept her*

*from that. It was that one should die naturally. Her pleas, "I want to die" meant "I wish nature would kill me."*

*Why, or what is it that says that we must let nature take its course? Has God made cowards of us? Has my religious teaching – suicide a mortal sin, - scared me and made me a coward?*

*I always admired my brother who said to me with his eyes (as his stroke robbed him of his voice) "I'm going to die" and from that moment on he did by refusing food and drink. Is that not a slow suicide? Instead of ingesting a pill you refuse to eat or drink – the result is an act of the will, a killing of oneself.*

*If there is a God, would not the God say, "don't depend on me, grow up if you can; don't live in fear of me, take charge of your own life and decisions, even your last decision – death.*

*But on the other hand, am I just afraid of feebleness, despondency? Do I just abhor needing to be dependent on others, abhor being helpless? Should I not suffer the humiliation of peeing and pooping in bed?*

*Thinking this way it seems clear that the human, dignified, courageous, adult thing to do, is to be adult, responsible for my death if I have the opportunity. Of course a massive heart attack that kills me would relieve me of all this sweaty thinking.*

*I feel fragile, afraid in some way. I think of ending my life when the time comes. Then the specter of God enters my mind. What is right or wrong? That scares me to be "Wrong." Would I not be freer if I were like a friend of mine who is an atheist? He seems so free, has figured out his own code of ethics and it is very good!*

*In my grieving I've had a taste of agnosticism and it was liberating. I felt more totally responsible for all my actions for now and in the future.*

*Is sickness, feebleness a part of spiritual growth? Perhaps it is a challenge just to surrender, if in that brings spiritual growth. As I begin to fade, what is wrong with just ending life? On the other hand if I lived being dependent, perhaps I would be an opportunity for someone to love me. Are the sick and feeble only stimuli for others to grow in love? But is it growth for the feeble? Has not life lost it dignity?*

*Is it not more dignified to be courageous and end one's life when the end has arrived and one's only usefulness is perhaps to be an agent for someone else to grow in loving by caring for the sick and dying?*

Journal May 26, 2007- A month later after seeing the movie <u>Away From Her</u> the following came to me

*Funny - I've not had much to journal about lately. No deep or consequential thoughts and feelings came to me. For some reason, after reading the movie review of <u>Away From Her</u>, I immediately wanted to see it.*

*I thought I would cry when I would see it, but for some reason I didn't. I was not that sad, yet I was totally engaged. The movie was more like inviting me into a deep meditation on love and the slow dying of the loved one. [The movie and its superb actors depicted the slow, painful journey of the husband (Gordon Pinsent) losing his beloved wife (Julie Christie) to Alzheimer's.] I sat there comparing my experience to his. I accepted Anne's dying and death; he struggled with accepting it. He also struggled with how to love her when she disappeared mentally and in spirit from him and became attached, almost like animals do, to the closest object of affection in the nursing home - to another man. It was like his wife was reduced to only needing affection and getting it by giving it to another man in the home, – quite like animal Daphne does with me and I to her.*

*I went to bed last night somewhat disappointed that I did not seem more powerfully moved emotionally and*

*mentally by the movie. But I was wrong. When I woke this morning the following was clear to me.*

*I faced more clearly that I am slowly dying, even though it is by inches now, but will increase by feet sometime down the line. The signs of this – more bodily aches and pains, less energy, less ability to multitask, more easily distracted, more mistakes in spelling, diminished interest in playing golf.*

*I must prepare better for my dying the worst possible death, which would be losing my mind, – and only living in the mortal flesh. But to do that I must free myself from God as I understand that "God". I must grow up and take <u>full</u> responsibility for my life, which includes my death. Modern science, while benefiting us, has perhaps crippled us. It has allowed our mind to slip away while keeping the flesh alive. What good is that, to be returned to the animal state? When the mind goes, so should the body it seems to me. There should be a harmony there, integration. Anne worried that when her spirit wanted to die, the body wouldn't follow suit. She went to a healer to be integrated. I don't know if that helped or not. Anne believed in it, and so in that fashion I think it helped her.*

*No, I must now, more than ever, make sure that when my mind goes everything goes right with it. Pills, Hemlock Society, ability to decide not to eat or drink- I must figure all this out.*

*Has God revealed something to us about this? If Jesus is supposed to be <u>the</u> revelation of God to us, – what is there in that Jesus story that speaks to, validates my taking responsibility for my dying and ending my life?*

*The only thing I can think of is that Jesus clearly knew that his actions in the final days would bring about his death. His prayer in the Garden testifies to that. He was on a self-inflicted mission to be killed by the way he was living. Caiaphas had said "it would be better to their interest if one man died for the whole people", John 18:14.*

*Jesus knew it was better for him to die for the sake of humanity –to teach by dying that love is the greatest thing there is. Love is greater than life itself. Loving others is higher than living on and on and on. But what strikes me now is that Jesus was no dumbbell, he knew exactly what his actions would bring about – namely his death. He chose freely to end his life for the sake of others. Even theology puts the spin on this very cleverly – "He died for our sins" – as if putting it this way justifies his taking his own life, for surely he died knowing that <u>his freely chosen actions</u> would cause his death – like taking a pill does.*

*Instead of all this theological spin – "He died for our sins", why not just call the shots as it is – Jesus stood up to the ruling powers and the State executed him. And Jesus knew full well this would happen; therefore he freely chose to take actions that resulted in his death. Peter saw it coming and wanted to stop Jesus, but Jesus said – put away your sword.*

*So if I can no longer love others, love the world, offer something to the well being of human life, why not take action, a pill, ending my life and give my money and assets to helping those less fortunate, who have a life ahead of them to live and love for others. Why not love others by giving all away rather than spending it all in just keeping my body moving like a robot? As I write, this seems so stupid – to waste money so I can be a body without a spirit.*

*I now think I am getting clearer, more courageous, about when I can't love anymore, help anymore. I can die and let my earthly possessions help others.*

*I think this was also the dilemma posed by <u>Away From Here.</u> Julie Christie had the guts to decide to go to the Home where she would some day have her body finally waste away long after her mind had disappeared, but she never had the guts to put a time line on when to shut down completely.*

> *I must take responsibility and lay the markers down for myself when to end my life.*

One of the arguments used against my thinking here is that we must not interfere with nature. Let nature take its course. Yet we interfere with nature repeatedly by the injection of medicines, chemicals. In my family culture there was a saying, "pneumonia is the best friend of old people." Of course that piece of wisdom was bantered about in the 1930's when I was in grade school. I haven't heard it lately. Modern medicine is constantly interfering with the course of nature by developing more and more drugs and procedures to keep us alive.

This interruption of nature in some cases helps one to live more enjoyably and productively. This is considered good and moral. So it is moral to interfere in the course of nature. Why is it not moral to interfere to bring about death when one's life is no longer productive and enjoyable?

At last we have come to the point that we can tell the medical system not to apply "life sustaining processes" when we are seriously injured or sick and dying. Now we are encouraged to fill out a statement setting forth the conditions upon which we want no life sustaining interventions.

Journal - The following month my thinking continues, June 11, 2007

> *I think my entry today will be the email I sent to my friend. It reflects my ongoing struggle in my mind and soul.*

> Dear _____,
> *I'm now reading the book, <u>Blessed Unrest</u> by Paul Hawken. Here is a quote from page 25 - "Evolution is not about design or will; it is the outcome of constant endeavors made by organisms that want to survive and better themselves." – from Michael Pollan's, <u>Botany of Desire: A Plant's Eye View of the World</u>.*

*Now while that applies to plants primarily, I think, in what way does it have application to humans who have the power to design and to make decisions? We too are organisms even though we also have these two powers that plants lack. Hawken is making the point that we also will evolve, not from super powers and organizations, but more from individuals on this planet struggling to survive and better themselves.*

*The question before me is what is the meaning of "bettering ourselves". What is better for humans, just to let one's body finally shut down on its own, or to use design and will to either stop the shutting down or to enhance the shutting down? There is no question that enormous effort has been put into lengthening life. So people in the "developed" world, that consumes most of the earth's resources out of proportion to the number of people on earth today, now can live longer using up our resources in a disproportionate way. But considering this global picture has little impact on me who wants to live another day. If a doc said he had a pill that would lengthen my life in good health for 30 more years (till 111 years of age), ought I, would I, take it? Should I even be thinking of such questions? Is it just a waste of time?*

*Yours truly in the state of "But what do I know?",*
*Bill*

*P.S. Yes, basically life is a mystery - but then why did God, if there is such a being, give us this damn mind whereby we are humanly driven to use it??? It just creates confusion and stress in poor creatures like me. "Down With Thinking - Rest in Authority" could be a new movement I'll start.*

## Journal February 14, 2008

*I just read my entry from 5/26/07. It is so clear about being responsible for one's death. I had forgotten that I had written this and was so clear about it. It so relieves me reading this; it makes so much sense to me today. It's like I don't need to struggle with the thinking about it any more. It is so clear to me. All I need to do is make my plans.*

Is it not ironical that currently I am involved in an effort to gather signatures on an Initiative here in Washington State to put on November's ballot a "Death With Dignity" law similar to the one in Oregon? This campaign is led by one of our former Governors who has Parkinson's disease. I would have done this even before Anne's melanoma, but after these last two and half years I am more convinced of the value of this legislation to offer the freedom to those who wish to have a doctor place pills on the bedside of one dying who wishes to take them to end one's life.

I am also aware that even though this last entry of February 14, 2008 reflects a stronger conviction about being responsible for my dying as well as my living, at times there are moments when doubt, indecision enters my mind. I suspect that when the time comes, I'll just trust my feelings, my intuition. I just hope my weakened mind or some fear will not obstruct that intuition.

CHAPTER 18

# Do I Want Another Love?

OVER the last two and a half years since Anne died, my Journal reflects my pondering over whether or not I would ever want to be married to another woman. It reveals my developing attitude about this.

Journal December 25, 2005 about 10 weeks after Anne died

*Yesterday a seemingly new thought occurred to me. I not only missed Anne being with me and for me, but I missed not have someone to love day in and day out. I missed not having the joy of loving just one other special person, as with Anne. I feared losing my capacity to love unselfishly.*

*This new realization of lacking someone to love was a different feeling as compared to my past feeling of sadness in missing Anne. When I miss not being able to love someone I am missing not being the actor rather than the victim. I miss being able to devote my life, my caring, my loving to another. I miss not loving in that total, special, one on one way that grew so strong the last year. I miss the feeling of disappearing into one other person. I miss not being absorbed in a way in which I became nothing and she became everything. It's more than that. I miss losing myself in her to become one with her with the result of feeling larger than self, though not in an egotistical sense.*

*It was like being one in Anne. In totally loving Anne I experience something new. It is hard to explain.*

*As I think about what I have just written, I can see that I was somewhat referring to this new awareness when I wrote earlier in this journal that I feared that my love, that had been so purified during the 10 months of her dying, would be lost without Anne to love. I feared that I would return to me and become self-centered. What came to me yesterday was not that kind of fear, but simply not having anyone to give myself to totally; to be completely absorbed in another that results in being enlarged. It wasn't even about Anne and me, it was about a new reality, a new phenomenon that in itself was something I can't describe any better than to use the word <u>Love</u>, as if that love has a transcendent personality to it.*

*I miss having someone in my life to love. I miss not only what Anne gave and meant to me, but I now miss not having her here so I can love her, give myself to her fully.*

Six months elapse before the next entry on this subject occurs.

## Journal May 1, 2006 Six and half month after Anne's death

*I thought I would be over the loneliness to some degree by now. In fact I thought I had, but in the last few days missing Anne has re-emerged as strongly as before. I think of what a friend of mine who had lost his wife several years ago told me in Germany in March. He said that after six months he felt a certain freedom. It was a freedom that allowed him to meet and now be with a special companion. I am not sure what kind of freedom it was from. Was it from his first wife? From what? Could it be that I will never experience that "freedom" since I am so in love with Anne? I just can't conceive of anyone like her. Besides would it be fair to get connected to someone else with the love in my heart for Anne? I think I will probably be like another friend's father who so loved his wife that for 14 years after her death he never remarried or got intimate with another woman. I must admit it is not a satisfying picture of the future.*

*But for now, the thought of marrying someone seems so distant from me.*

### Journal - The next day, May 2, 2006

*So what if I will never be happy, lively, as I was with Anne? Perhaps I should just accept that and make the most of the life given to me.*

*I fear, though, that by living alone as I am I will slip away from the unselfish love I had obtained with Anne the last year of her life. I hate thinking of that happening. But, if by living alone, I am preoccupied with me, my duties of staying alive, eating, taking care of the house, etc. do I not become the object of my own attention? Do I not become self-full, if not selfish?*

*With Anne, in her sickness of cancer, she became the total object of my life. I vanished into her...*

*For now until new insights and ways are opened to me, I guess I'll just accept the small good I can do and the lesser happiness that I have. Just accept the lower life for now.*

### Journal July 6, 2007

*A thought has been emerging within me the last several days. It has at last become clear – and it is so simple and obvious that I am almost embarrassed to write it.*

*As I have been living alone since Anne died I have had no live person present to me 24 hours around the clock; a person present to me whose presence challenges, or better, beckons love from me. Living with a person, such as a spouse or loved one, is a constant invitation to be thoughtful, considerate, helpful, giving in myriad ways.*

*Yes, it is only an invitation. I could live with a person and be essentially self-centered rather than other centered. However without such a person with whom intimacy is part of the relationship, I can grow out of practice in being loving and generous.*

*Another thought – the presence 24 hours from another is an invisible, unconscious almost constant stimulation of liveliness. Two live energies bouncing off each other, stimulating each other. Not having that now, I am more aware of this stimulation I had for 23 years. Lack of stimulation quickens death; or at least is a death like experience.*

*How am I to cope with this situation, this lack of a daily invitation to love, this lack of daily stimulation which is life giving?*

## Journal - March 16, 2008, Two years and five months since Anne died

*I am aware that in the last three or four evenings I grew more tired of eating alone than I can remember. I longed for the stimulation of eating with a trusted person.*

*Then this morning as I awoke, I was clear about two things. One, I was not feeling sad about missing Anne so much the last month; and two, I was definitely missing someone to whom I could extend my love. I both fear and miss not having someone to love. I could pour out my attention, caring, giving – to make the other the focus of my attention rather than me. I have this capacity to love; it is a shame I'm not gifting someone with it.*

*Yet do I want to spend the time, energy in dealing with our differences? I think that if I met, or let my eyes be open to what is already in my circle of acquaintances, I might connect to the right person as I did to Anne. My gut would tell me that it would not be that difficult to grow into intimacy with another.*

*Is it possible to carry two loves in me, that of Anne and of the other? If Anne is fused with me, is it possible that she and I could love another intimately? Would this be betraying my love of Anne?*

*Perhaps if Anne lives in me, she will find someone for me. Silly thought? Make believe? I don't think so, for I've had the experience of our love that joined us, fused us as one – and I have the feeling, experience that it is still there somehow.*

*I could lean upon my ability to love Anne as a newly acquired gift to be given away to another.*

Shortly after this entry I had a quick moment of a dream. A woman was leaning over me, gently kissing me. I woke with a welcoming smile on my face. I felt more open to the possibility of someone new in my life, but even as I write this I feel a tinge of fear in me. I can't put my finger on precisely what I am fearing. Betraying Anne? The impossibility of this ever happening? But is spite of the fear, I still feel the warmth of the kissing and my smiling.

CHAPTER 19

# Special Reflections and Events

**IN** this chapter, I share some events and reflections that were significant to me in my life after Anne.

### FEAST DAYS IN GRIEVING

The following entry describes my first Christmas after Anne died. It symbolizes the poignancy of such special days in my life after Anne.

Journal December 23, 2005, 3:30 a.m.

*Well I just can't sleep. I've tossed and thought, for it seems like about an hour. So I surrender, I get this pad and pen and now am writing in the bed at 3:30 in the morning. I shut the window so it will not be too cold around the shoulders.*

*Last night after dinner, on almost automatic pilot mode, I start to clear spaces in the house for Christmas decorations. I clean the dining room buffet to lay the clean white folded bed sheet on top of the long buffet. I'm preparing the space for the crèche – as I've done every Christmas. It is the beautiful simple statue figures of Mary, Joseph, Baby Jesus, Shepherds, Sheep, and Three Wise Men with their gifts. I have cherished this simple tan clay set of small statue figures for years. Anne cherished it too as I brought this part of Christmas to our life together.*

*I go to the garage, get the box of these small statues.*

*I place candles around the figures and on the windowsills. It will be so nice when my friends come to dinner tomorrow night. I now become aware, that in doing all this I am feeling sad. The low-grade sadness seems to be with me all the time but now I am beginning to be aware of it. But the awareness is slight as I go about my business of decorating the dinning room. I feel a satisfaction with the crèche in place; even light all the candles just to see how it will look. I'm satisfied, feel some pride and joy.*

*Now back to the garage to decide whether to get the small trunk upon which to put the Christmas tree. I decide in favor of doing it. Then I begin to look for the beautiful red drape cloth that Anne had to put on the trunk. I opened the closet door in the garage and see all the boxes, all the loose decorations for Christmas and I am overwhelmed. At first it's the task of plowing through all those boxes that overwhelms me – and then suddenly I feel overwhelmed by sadness. Sadness in doing all this without Anne, sadness in just missing her, sadness that she's not here to enjoy doing this too, for if anything, Anne got the biggest kick out of "doing Christmas" - the lights over the door and windows – wreaths on the door and over the mantle – lights galore – decorations galore – a festival coming alive to live in our abode for days on end. My sadness was deeply felt.*

*Then I noticed something that has become clearer to me the last several weeks. Sadness zaps energy from me. As I felt my deep sadness, I felt a definite sucking of energy from my body. I had to stop. I closed the garage closet doors slowly, left the garage, and said to myself "I can't do anymore, I'll wait until tomorrow morning." I then prepared for bed, filling our wonderful jet tub with water and salts to soak and prepare for bed. At 11 PM, turned out the lights and went to sleep.*

*Now it's 3:55 a.m. and about five minutes ago I heard Daphne from her kennel in the kitchen. Strange, last night when I put her in her "safety net" I did not fasten the gate door as I always do. I said to myself, I'll just close it and leave it unfastened to see what she might do. And now here she is, looking at me, head at the side of the bed with her expressive face and big brown eyes as if to say, "Are you okay Bill?" I pet her and pet her until she slumps down on the floor beside me.*

*She has been the most tender, gentle and loving companion in our lives, and lots of fun to play with, walk with, and throw the ball. Hardly a day goes by that she doesn't make me laugh by antics she pulls off. She's staring at me from the lying position on the floor. The house would be hell to live in without her.*

*The living room clock just chimed 4 a.m. I feel better now – alive, refreshed in having written this. I've expressed love and the love soothes my saddened soul. I'll turn out the light and see what happens.*

Letters to Anne

About four months after Anne's death, February 12, 2006, I found myself beginning to write letters to her. Since then I have written several letters to her. This is the first that I wrote.

*Oh Anne,*
*This is the first time it has come to me to write to you.*
*I just want to tell you how much I miss you. I miss you so much. If I could be assured that we would have a life together after body death, then I would seriously contemplate ending my body life to be with you.*
*Nothing so far, since your death, compares to my life with you. There is that certain zest missing no matter how wonderful I try to make my life. All during the past week I was thinking of you, missing you.*
*I wonder if this present feeling will change. There is a way in which I don't want it to change. Missing you, feeling the sadness of that is a way for me to be with you.*

*You are present to me in my state of sadness and loneliness stemming from my memories of you and knowing you are not with me in body – in the form I knew you and enjoyed your presence in my life.*

*If I stop missing you, with its attendant feelings, will then you not disappear from me? That I do not want. That I fear.*

*How will this journey of grief end for me? Will it be transformed so that I do not lose sight of you, yet not have the sadness? Will it be transformed so that I retain strong memories of you, but not accompanied by the feeling of loneliness? Will it be transformed so that I once again have the zest and joie de vivre that I had with you?*

*If so, then what part do I play in that transformation? Or do I play any part? Does it just happen? How does it just happen? Is it one of those gifts, graces, from God?*

*Or, what am I doing? Am I not staying in the here and now? Am I not following the dictum of Nkosi Johnson – "do all you can with what you have, in the time you have, in the place you are in."*[3]

*But who says that in the moment I am thinking of you, I am in the remembering of you I am writing this note to you – that I am not living in the here and now "doing all I can…" If living in the here and now means I am never to think of you, remember you, remember our past moments of joy – then that means you vanish from me. That doesn't seem to make sense to me.*

*This Sunday morning in Gig Harbor the sun is out, the beauty of the world is full of Northwest splendor as I write this and look out my windows. It was in enjoying nature's beauty that I felt the enthusiasm of wanting to write this to you, the first direct note to you since 10/14. What does this mean?*

*My most absolute love,*

---

[3] Nkosi Johnson was a South African child who died of AIDS at age of 12

*Bill – P.S. As soon as I wrote "absolute", it came to me that you are part of the God.*

## THE ROLE OF FAMILY ROOTS IN MY LIFE

In this period of my life after Anne, I found myself returning to reflecting upon my roots in various ways. These moments always brought a sense of peace and satisfaction to me. It gave me a sense of strength in that moment. Here is an example of these reflections.

This took place on a bumpy bus ride to Heathrow Airport in London after teaching a class in the UK. It is recorded by my Journal entry written on December 4, 2006 - 9:45a.m., a year and two months after Anne.

*My mind wanders to my grandmother. Interesting – I lived with her and Papa for three years when I was 10 -13 years old, while my parents separated. I have certain memories of her, but not many details of our living together.*

*As I try to recapture some of the memories, I puzzle why I don't remember the flow of my life with them, I remember the flow of my life, but not with them so much.*

*Two explanations come to me – I lived from day to day more in the duties and fun of the present moment. My life was given to me and as such I dealt with it on a daily basis – never complaining, never wishing for a different life. This is the way it was and it made sense. Daily routine was clearly marked. Go to school, do the best you can to pass, serve Mass as an altar boy, play sports, sell newspapers and ponder over the different personalities of my playmates, help grandmother, play pinochle with them – cope with my inadequacies, always trying to improve whether it was pitching softball or passing a test. I just lived from day to day with the security that life handed to me.*

*The other explanation was that my grandmother was simply a securing, peaceful, noninvasive presence to me; she was more of an atmosphere I lived in – loving, supportive and letting me discover my own path in life from day to day within a structured environment with certain basic rules and expectations and meanings, which I more simply absorbed than was told.*

*I accepted those rules and meanings without doubt, resistance or desire for anything else. Be obedient and good. Try to enjoy as much as possible of life and do my duties. The markers were clear and within these markers I had the space to design and forge my life. I became resourceful, independent and responsible. I can't remember being scolded, frowned upon or told what to do except to run errands. I must have been told what to do – but I don't remember. It seemed like I gathered what was expected and I did it.*

*My grandmother, Cordelia LeGarde Rodier from Quebec is the only person I have regarded as truly a saint. A saint means to me a person who is so much in touch with the spiritual realm of reality that her wisdom and love, beauty and goodness transcends the normal realities we humans live with and are accustomed to. There was nothing she said or did that was so important or impressive – it simply was her presence! Her presence changed the environment, changed the world around her, not in some "pietistic" sense, but in the sense that life was fully lived with peace and gusto! Could this presence of my grandmother from 10 to 13 years of age be the real explanation of my belief in God? Was not the presence of my grandmother the presence of God?*

## DISPOSING OF ANNE'S POSSESSIONS.

I have been slow in disposing Anne's possessions. I kept her clothes in her bedroom closet for eight months. Somehow, it comforted me. It was a symbol, a presence of Anne for me.

But one day I thought how those clothes, shoes, coats, hats could benefit others. Once that thought came to me, it was easy for me to decide to give it away.

The top of Anne's dresser still has all the things that she put there such as pictures of her boys and grandkids, while the drawers beneath are now empty. A small quilt, made and given to her by one of the groups she belonged to, is neatly folded on Anne's side of the bed. These things comfort me. They make the bedroom warm and alive for me.

I know that some bereaved spouses immediately dispose of all such artifacts as it helps them deal with the pain of their loss. Some even sell their homes soon after the death. This is an example of the different ways each of us deals with the death of a loved one.

I try to be careful not to let my attachment to Anne interfere with my life. I try to integrate it into my on-going life. I am open to admit that what I am doing may not be the best road to follow. For years I have a pendant hanging around my neck containing five small diamonds, one given by my father to my mother when I was born, one from my favorite aunt and three from my sister— and I wear my brother's Movado watch. All of them are deceased. Now I have attached a locket with some of Anne's ashes to the pendant. So, in a sense I carry my family roots and Anne with me.

I do believe loving energy is residual. I will never forget an experience I had back in the 70's. On a Monday morning, I went out to see the pyramids at the ancient ruins of Teotihuacán 30 miles northeast of Mexico City. There were very few visitors, mainly merchants setting up their kiosks. I passed through the ring of kiosks and walked toward the pyramids. As I walked closer, I felt some sort of a new atmosphere or energy hitting me. This took me aback. It created a sense of being in a holy place. I just stopped, and gazed and enjoyed the sacredness of it all. A student of anthropology then told me this is a common experience for people.

The only sense I made of this is that those who built these

pyramids were doing so out of their religious or spiritual faith. It must have taken many years to construct these huge structures. And that spiritual energy remained in that space. I had the same experience when I visited Lourdes at the afternoon Benediction of the Blessed Sacrament where some 10,000 people walked in the open space in silence and the volunteers were carrying the sick on stretchers to the ceremony. It was as if the energy snapped me into a spiritual mode. I felt an enormous energy of love for the sick.

## THE IMPACT OF A HABIT OF LIFE BEING BROKEN

It amazes me how I have never considered some simple realities of life. I am almost embarrassed to admit the following insight was a new one for me; the truth of it is so obvious but it never dawned on me with such power. It is dealt with in this Journal entry April 8, 2007, Easter Sunday almost a year and half after Anne died.

*I woke up and didn't want to get out of bed at my usual 6 a.m. So I stayed till around 7 o'clock. I felt confused, without answers, direction – and again "what am I living for?" I tried what worked in the past – "be grateful for each moment; live in the moment" – it didn't help. It didn't relieve my confusion, my trying to make sense of my life, or just getting out of bed.*

*I thought of today's feast, the Resurrection. That didn't help either. It was almost like not wanting to go there.*

*I thought about my love, the result of my loving – Anne in me and I'm in her. But that felt flat, meaningless. If she is in me, why don't I experience that, experience her? I felt empty – she wasn't in me. So have all these writings and thoughts about Anne living in me and I in her been just the ramblings of a person who is living in make-believe-land? If we are still one, so what, - it offers me no life, no spark, - it leaves me empty.*

*The women go to the tomb; they find it empty. I go to my heart and find it empty. My grief intensifies; I feel sharply my loss.*

*Then the thought – let go, don't try to make sense, don't try to change my state of mind and feeling. Just surrender.*

*I thought of Anne finally throwing her pen and yellow pad down when she was trying to track the results of new medication that the Hospice nurse was going to give her. Anne, being the one who always had to know so much about anything concerning her life, simply smiled and said, "I don't need to know anymore", with relief in her body and face. That was a marked moment in her journey to death. We all laughed with Anne and cheered the breakthrough with her.*

*Should I not try to take control of my living or just let everything go, just die? There is something very appealing about that, as I seem so immersed in the dull, boring duties of just living. Yet, if I am given this life to live, am I not betraying something sacred in not trying to live the best I can – for whatever purposeless reason?*

*As I write this, I look out the window. The scene of nature with the emerging sun is beautiful, but I don't seem to enjoy it. I'm not thrilled by it. I get little pleasure from God's beauty this morning.*

*Then, at last, a new thought comes to me, one I haven't really considered. Anne's death broke, ended a habit of life I had for 23 years with her. It was a habit of where everything in my life, from getting up or staying in bed, from observing the beauty of Spring's budding colors, to even writing in a journal – was done with somehow Anne being in and a part of my life. She was in a part of every single moment of my existence, even though I may be in Europe engrossed in teaching, in some way she was part of my life. And her being part of my existence, made my existence zestful, at times challenging.*

*That 23 years habit of life was shattered at her death.*

*I am not used to my new emerging habit of living without her. I must give myself more time to enter into it as best I can.*

## THE IMPORTANCE OF TRUST

In my journey of life after Anne's death, I have learned something that I had never considered so deeply before in my life, namely the absolute value and role of trust in our lives. This entry on January 26, 2007 (15 months after Anne died), my 81st birthday, reflects this special learning.

*My mind wanders to our final goodbye on 10/3/05, (six days before her seizure) which I recorded on my iPod. Anne simply begins speaking without any provocation from me. She says that due to her earlier experience, she could never trust a man again and would never love a man again. But knowing me first as a friend, she could begin to trust me and that allowed her to love me.*

*That opening statement of Anne's has stuck with me for some reason.*

*It was only this morning that it struck me that trusting another completely, and then having that trust broken, is such a severe shock to one's system. It occurred to me, what a high value, human reality, trust is in our lives.*

*I realize that trust probably carries different importance to different people. But does it? How can one fully love, give oneself to another so much as to become one with that person without first trusting that person? How can you place yourself unreservedly into the hands of another without a deep trust of that person? And so when you do allow love to grow and flower based on this trust, it comes as a tremendous shock to feel betrayed.*

*Perhaps the ability to trust is one of the toughest human achievements. Could that be due to the fact we experience our own fallibility, so it is difficult to trust the other? That is, if we can't trust ourselves since we are fallible, how can we trust another? I think that Anne honored trust so highly because she was such a faithful keeper of her own word.*

*So as I reflect on this, this morning, I am more deeply touched by how she trusted me not to betray her. She could finally come to trust and love a man, me.*

*What a nice birthday gift to me to <u>realize</u> that she could trust me. My mother once told me that no man ever respected and loved her so much as my father. Did I not get this from my father? Thank you W.F.*

*I feel good about myself on my 81st birthday and about my fidelity that allowed my Anne to trust and love me. Perhaps my life is worthwhile after all.*

If trust is the precondition for someone to love another, give oneself totally to another, then what a tremendous thing trusting is.

This brings me back to the chapter on mystery and the disappearance of God in my life. It makes clearer to me that "faith" is not so much holding on to something for which there is no proof, but rather "faith" is simply trusting. It is an experience as I tried to describe in the chapter on living in mystery. I know that I don't know. I know that what I know pales in comparison to what I don't know; that I live mostly in a world of mystery and uncertainty. And somehow if I <u>experience trusting the very mystery I dwell in,</u> that may be what "faith in God" is all about! I don't arrive at this experience through logic or proof; I either have it or not. I suspect that the story of Job in the Old Testament is about this very issue. In spite of all the trials and tribulations he experienced he rather, unreasonably, still trusted God.

I think to be able to trust another completely one must be able to trust oneself in spite of our human frailties.

## THE EXPERIENCE OF BEING ABSOLUTELY LIFELESS.

This entry of September 8, 2007, almost two years since Anne died, tells of a remarkable experience I had.

*I awoke this morning @ 5:30, eyes still burning. I got up, but felt tired and went back to bed. A variety of images, thoughts went through my mind. In the midst of the disconnected flow of thoughts, I felt a moment of having no energy at all.*

*I felt like if this is all that's left in me, I want to die. This lack of energy was so strong that I felt I could do nothing. It was a moment of lifelessness as it were.*

*Simply wanting to die was OK. This feeling was different than not wanting to get up to face the day's dull chores. It was different from not having a life-giving meaning that urges me out of bed – as bad as that feeling is. No, it was just simply an experience of being energy-less, lifeless. I can't recall ever having this experience before. It was an experience devoid of any feeling.*

*I was quite content just to die and be with Anne, or be content to vanish into nothingness if that's the fate of death.*

*This moment passed rather quickly. I then felt grateful. I think I experienced what Anne was going through those few days before she went into her seizure-coma when she uttered several times to me that she wanted to die. I also felt grateful for this experience as it deepened my understanding how it will come to me to want to die and that it is not only okay but is also a contented, peaceful feeling – it's time to go. This experience gave me a sense of security and lack of fear for my own death when it is time.*

## THE JOY OF CONTEMPLATION

One of the benefits of living alone these days is that I seem to live deeper inside myself. It is easier to be in a meditative space. My missing Anne helps me slow down. In fact, I enjoy this slow walking through life, undistracted, in contemplation of what is around me and in me.

I see my stepsons and families preoccupied with their kids,

their work, their goings and comings – a life of details, duties, and distractions – much like mine when Anne was alive and before I retired from being a therapist. Almost every year in my marriage, I felt a need to take off for several days just to be by myself, to enter into myself. It always refreshed me. Anne encouraged me in doing this.

Now this is reversed. I live more like a monk and need to seek outside contacts and activities. But I enjoy living more in the spirit than in concreteness of activities.

One experience that I had highlights my comfort in contemplating. On December 17, 2006, I returned home from being out of town. A terrific windstorm had hit the Seattle–Tacoma area knocking out electricity, toppling trees, blocking roads. I was unaware of this until the shuttle picked me up at the airport and I noticed all the lights outside the airport were off including traffic signals.

As I turned into my driveway, two huge pine trees had blown over my driveway so that I could not drive into the garage. I parked the car on the street, barely was able to climb over the trees with my luggage and made my way into the house. I figured I had about three hours of daylight to get Daphne from the Kennel where she had been boarded and to prepare the house for my night of darkness. I lived without water, heat, phone and electricity for three days. It was a special moment for me as stated in the following entry.

*From 4:30 p.m. to 7:30 p.m. on Friday night I have been living in darkness. I can't read, distract myself with music or TV. I went to bed at 7:00p.m. I just lay there with nothing to do but think. I let my mind free associate, go wherever it wanted to. Then at times I tried to control my mind, focus it on some subject. I preferred the free association – less work and energy expended.*

*Saturday night I was invited to dinner and Scrabble with friends who had electricity. I went to bed a 10:30p.m., but wide-awake. The same as Friday night; I just laid there quiet in the darkness. I fell asleep that way.*

*I think this enforced darkness, quiet mind, with nothing to do, to read, to look at, brought this deepened experience as I awoke Sunday morning. I thought: we evolve. We evolved from the helpless infant that we were to the aged, experienced person, of many accomplishments, achieving wisdom and love along the way. The whole of creation is one of evolving. This evolving goes on through cycles of living and dying. Even facing death itself is part of the evolving process.*

*Given that, how can it be that death is the total ending? Such an ending would be contrary to everything in our universe and everything in our own personal life's experience. Even the body's diminishment is evolution's way of getting the spirit, mind, whatever you wish to call it, ready to move on to the next stage of evolving.*

*This line of thinking supports my trust that all of us in dying in the body are evolving into a new life experience whatever that might be. Some call it heaven; others call it the Beatific Vision, being one with God.*

*All these thoughts bubbling up from the depths of darkness these past two nights made me more confident in being okay with dying.*

*My mind flashes to my grandmother's death. It was, what I would call, the holiest death in my life.*

*On her bed of dying, she called all of her living adult sons and daughters to her bedside one by one and gave each a final statement. Then she called them all in including Papa. With her bed surrounded by her husband and sons and daughters, she closed her eyes, a smile appeared on her face, a single tear dropped from each closed eye and she died with a smile on her face. I believe she faced the God she had come to love with her whole heart and soul. She had transcended.*

I did not write this in my journal but to this day, I remember that on Sunday when all power and water was restored, I felt I was losing something. I was disappointed that the darkness was over. I had come to embrace and enjoy it. I had enjoyed the silence and deprivation of distractions! I could no longer distract myself. I had to live in the poverty of my surroundings and this led me deeper into my soul. I loved it.

### THE EMERGENCE OF POETRY WITHIN ME.

In the last several months I found myself writing what might be called poems. Perhaps earlier in my life I might have written a poem or two, but I can't remember. I was surprised by this new experience and don't know where it came from. Here is one written December 7, 2007.

### Time Becoming Short

*The signs began to appear -*
*The signal went out -*
*Time is coming to an end.*

*I read, yet did not read, the signs.*
*She could only play nine holes,*
*Then four, then none.*

*She stopped having her wine with dinner.*
*She stopped listening to the news.*
*She took her last walk to the mailbox.*

*Her last walk was from her bed*
*To the living room couch,*
*She wanted to die, to die.*

*I knew time was running out.*
*But I considered not the future.*
*I just lived in the moment*

*Of her every breath -
And stayed alive myself.*

*Then finally she took her last breath;
It was over.
Half of me died with her.*

*It is fitting that now I feel
Only half alive. I accept it.*

CHAPTER 20

# Where From, Where To

As I began my life after Anne's death, I knew what might be in store for me from the books I had read on grieving. However, these were only ideas. The actual experience far surpasses the ideas, so much so that I hardly remember what the ideas were.

One of the ideas I do remember from early readings was that some experts on grieving cited anger as one of the stages everyone goes through. I am not surprised however that I still have not had any anger over Anne's death. I think our preparation for death over the years of our life together is the reason for this. Anne and I accepted death for what it is, part of life.

I think the major experience of my new life is a pervading sadness. It is conscious at times and unconscious the rest of the time. The second pervading experience is that my life simply is not as zestful as it was with Anne. Nothing has filled that lack of zest so far. Another way of putting this is that there is a decrease in enthusiasm in almost anything I do that in prior times I would have in abundance. Life alone is not as stimulating as life was with Anne.

So sadness and lack of zest have been the two most pervading feelings.

But the living alone, the sadness, and lack of enthusiasm somehow has enriched me. I think I may be a better person now.

It has allowed me to know what it's like to have loved so completely and lose that to death. Thus I can sympathize as never before with those who have lost loved ones.

It has slowed me down and allowed me to live each moment more openly and thoughtfully. For example, at checkout counters in stores I find myself taking the time to look into the checker's eyes, to smile, to offer gentle humorous one-liners, and to say with greater meaning "thank you" and "you too, have a good day." There is more of a softness in my voice.

It has allowed me to become much more contemplative, pondering mystery, nature and the world I live in. This contemplative tone in my life allows me to enter more deeply into my own self, to know myself better.

It has helped me to consult more with my friends to check out my own thinking, attitudes, judgments, interpretations of self, others and the world.

I find myself more open to accept what is given to me in each moment rather than trying to shape the moments by the activity of my mind and will. Never before has classical music, opera arias, and soulful music been in my background as now. Seldom do I listen to Sinatra, whereas with Anne we often did as we danced to it. The classical music and the music of Bach and other religious composers seem more congruent with my spirit these days.

I am much more willing to surrender to the mystery I live in, to what bubbles up in me to do. For example, I am content now just to lie in bed or on the couch and do nothing, think nothing – to enjoy a blank mind, a blank space. I see this as a gift whereas before I would view it as wasting time. I'm willing to live in the blank space and see what happens.

The occasions that remind me of Anne, resulting in sharp pains of missing her, are less frequent. The feeling of sadness is not as heavy as it was in the beginning, even though there will be short moments of deep heaviness even now.

I would never have predicted the journey I have taken with God and with my views about death and dying as revealed in chapters 14 and 17. What is even more important is that I feel more empowered in my agnostic position and more courageous in taking responsibility for how I die.

I live in serenity and peace at this time. I trust the force of nature and life and this mystery in which I am embedded. I trust in not knowing, or in having to know.

I sense the residual energy of love in this house.

While I can magically wish a resurrection of Anne, I welcome my life as is, even though lacking much, and want to learn more from it.

I do find excitement in realizing that I live more in the unknown and willing to be open to embrace whatever comes my way. As soon as I write this I think this sounds terribly passive. Why not take the reins and create a new future myself; would this not be acting as a responsible person? Yet, at this moment, at least, I feel more at peace in entering into each moment and letting the chain of moments create the future.

Lately I have also felt a certain excitement in returning to my life of activism after I finish this book.

It is Spring now in the Northwest, April is only five days away – Spring the time of new life, resurrection. What new life might come to me?

I feel very unfinished in my evolving.

I end with this Journal entry of November 11, 2007, two years and one month after Anne died

> *Oh, my dear Anne,*
>
> *I don't know why I'm writing you a letter. This is not my usual journal format. But earlier today I had this urge – just to be with you by writing.*
>
> *In wandering around this house on Sunday, I became acutely aware of missing you here. I felt like I had to write to tell you so. As soon as I thought of it I was puzzled by this desire.*
>
> *Then the duties of the day came upon me and I lost sight of this desire.*
>
> *But now again, I just want to write to you.*
>
> *It's like you are my only steady companion. You are not here, yet you are. I feel like writing you is better than*

*trying to talk to you. Talk ends shortly and abruptly, then no answer. This writing takes more time, more lingering with you as opposed to the quickly said sentence.*

*So as I write, a slower way, I am with you more. More time that allows more depth to the meaning, to the moment.*

*Why am I doing this? You do not see what I'm doing, yet in my very doing you seem to be with me. I don't feel so alone now; somehow you are with me – some sort of real presence. I can see your face, body – a memory, yes I know. But it almost seems more than a memory.*

*Oh, if I could only touch your body, feel your warmth – have your energy, bodily presence, but this is the best I can have.*

*Do you know, my dear, how much I love you? Ah, just writing that does something to me. I don't know what, but it feels good.*

*I love you and miss you and wish you were still here in body.*

*This morning as I awoke, I had some sort of dreaming, can't remember any details, but I remember the essence; I was becoming very selfish, at times feisty, sarcastic. I felt so bad. I knew that if you were still here, I would not be this way because I would be loving you and that would spill over into my body, my soul, my everything. And I'd be more loving to all that is outside of me. And knowing this loss of you, knowing this fear I had of behaving so surly, I grieved. I grieved not for losing you, but for losing a better part of me.*

*I'm tempted to say, save me. But I know that that is not the right statement. The statement is, Bill save yourself. Strive, without the stimulus of Anne at your side, to push yourself to be ever so loving and not so sarcastic or combative. Come to all things out of love, not out of converting or winning or changing – but out of loving.*

*Oh Anne, there are times like this that I feel like just dying and coming to you. Yet I respect the mystery of my health, my life, not knowing what it is for, but to be open to what I can give, what I can be of meaning for. Let it come to me; let it be. I'm open and I hurt. But the hurt has the atmosphere of containing my love, my love for you. Thank for just being you and your love for me. It opened my love for you. – for another human, so deeply. Thank you, - thank you.*

## Epilogue

# Four years and nearly three months since Anne died

### JOURNAL 1/4/10 MONDAY MORNING 6:30 A.M.

*I've now lost it. But at 4:30 a.m. in bed, awake or in dream, I experienced it for a moment, then, I lost it. I know that no words can ever describe it, do it justice. All I can say is that it was a moment of experiencing what seemed like just "pure" love, pure loving.*

*Being in that feeling, that experience, I feared nothing. I saw death as my welcomed visitor, to take me into this reality of pure loving.*

*Oh, how I wish my minute-to-minute life could be absorbed in this power, this energy of purely loving. In this experience, I had no fear and no enemies. I thought of those who irritate me, I could love them. I thought of those who more than just irritate me, and I could love them.*

*Then I thought of myself, so filled with selfish preoccupations, small mindedness, self-centeredness, moving from action to action - motivated by what? - survival? penny ante pleasures? I am so far from being centered in love, in loving. I have not been taken over by love as a 24-hour driving force in the bowels of my soul. I am still a neophyte. But, at last, I know who I am, where I am and how far I have yet to go. Now at 84, I think I have come to love myself with all my warts and defects.*

*I have tasted morsels of this kind of love, as this morning in bed, as in loving Anne on her road to death. Having tasted it; I trust it and know it is <u>the</u> ultimate reality to be achieved, - or is it just given? John in one of his letters in the New Testament finally put his finger on it - "God is love."*

*What explains this unspeakable, unprintable experience?*

*I had spent all afternoon yesterday looking into the files of my family roots. I came upon the news clipping of my grandmother's death and the picture of her. I stared at it. It was the face of a calm, pure love that provided a safe haven for me when young. It wasn't any particular act she did, it was just her presence and what exuded into the atmosphere around her that in some way simply told me how to be. It was the invisible message that only "pure" love can transmit. It is indescribable.*

*However, increasingly in these four plus years of living without Anne I have come to get a small insight into what this unearthly love is. And I trust it, I trust the mystery of it and I open myself to being overtaken by it.*

# About the Author

Bill Nerin's life before Anne was one of serving others as a Catholic priest in Oklahoma from 1951 to 1975. He was concerned about social justice. In the 60's, he spent time in Hattiesburg, Mississippi during the Federal trial against the county registrar for voter discrimination. Due to his early involvement in facilitating small groups to examine and change social systems and later his psychological studies at Columbia University, he thought seriously about the dynamics of the typical Catholic Parish. Was it doing enough? Catholics have a well-honed personal morality; do not lie, do not steal, do not commit adultery. What many lacked was a keen social conscience. His Bishop agreed.

He proposed a new kind of parish which would be limited to about 200 adults so that they could empower themselves by sharing their feelings and thoughts as they grew in trusting each other. After sermons, they would break into small groups to discuss their reactions and then share those with the larger group. This open sharing of the laity was based on one of the salient principles that emanated from the Vatican Council, which Pope John XXIII convened, namely, that God lives in the people. Thus if we were to hear the voice of God, we needed to hear from the people as well as from the clergy.

This new experimental parish, sanctioned by the Bishop in 1966, called the Community of John XXIII, would own no property or Church edifice but rent open space on Sunday mornings. The money the parishioners contributed would go to social causes such as FISH, supporting a Montessori Day Care Center in the heart of the poverty area in Oklahoma City, peace actions, etc. In the late 60's, the parishioners studied in depth the morality of the Vietnam War. As a result, some spent an entire year studying pacifism and the principles of a just war by St. Augustine. It was the first Catholic parish in the nation that refused to pay the phone tax designated for the Vietnam War.

Soon, some Protestants were attracted to the parish as well as invalidly married Catholics. The Eucharistic meal, being a symbol of the unity in the community, was open to all the members.

The Bishop who supported the parish died and the new Bishop told the Community that they must restrict the Eucharist only to validly married Catholics. The members met on four consecutive Sundays in their small groups and decided they could not refuse the symbol of unity to all the members. In February of 1975, the entire Community resigned from the jurisdiction of the Bishop.

Bill Nerin continued working as a family therapist. He was a student, then colleague, of the late Virginia Satir who was a leader in the field of family therapy. What drew him to her was her clear vision that emotional stress upon families and individuals that led to dysfunction was due to social conditions as much as to any individual defects. Thus to help people, one needed to treat not only the social system of the nuclear and extended family but also the larger society in which families lived.

In working with Virginia Satir, Bill first met Anne, a clinical psychologist, in the late 70s. In October 1982, Anne, 52 and Bill, 56 married and grew in love for 23 years until her death, October 14, 2005. Bill is an Adjunct Assistant Professor in the Human Relations Department at the University of Oklahoma, as was Anne. In 1986, Bill wrote his first book *Family Reconstruction: Long Day's Journey Into Light* and in 1993, *You Can't Grow Up Till You Go Back Home*.

What made their marriage so engaging and fulfilling was that they shared so much in common. Besides being therapists, they shared the same view of the world and sense of social justice. They loved to play golf, bridge and to dance to the same kind of music. They supported each other when fragile. Anne supported and aided Bill in writing his first two books and it is in her honor that he has dedicated this book.